If You're Reading These Words

Last Letters from Heroes of the October 7th War

Shlomo Kavas • Racheli Palant-Rozen

If you're reading these words

LAST LETTERS FROM HEROES
OF THE OCTOBER 7TH WAR

TRANSLATED BY
Sara Daniel

The Toby Press

If You're Reading These Words:
Last Letters from Heroes of the October 7th War

First English Edition, 2026

The Toby Press
An imprint of Koren Publishers Jerusalem Ltd.

POB 8531, New Milford, CT 06776-8531, USA
& POB 4044, Jerusalem 9104001, Israel
www.korenpub.com

Cover art: The drawing of the Magen David was copied from the last letter of Adi Leon z"l (see page 87). Courtesy of the Estate of Adi Leon

The publication of this book was made possible through the generous support of *The Jewish Book Trust*.

ISBN 978-1-59264-737-8, *paperback*

Printed in ROT

This book is sponsored by

The Weisfeld Family
Charitable Foundation

whose mission is to strengthen
Eretz Yisrael, Zionism, Jewish continuity,
and strong Jewish education for all

Netanya, Israel; Highland Beach, FL, USA;
and Toronto, Canada

Contents

Editors' Introduction

I'm writing this down here because I realize that the deadly battle we just got through isn't the last.

*

I hope – I'm sure – that later on, we'll read this letter together in the yard over some good beer and a cigarette and laugh.

*

Tension's in the air, and also dark humor about who will be coming back and who won't.

*

In case something happens to me, I have something to tell you.

*

Who's supposed to teach twenty-three-year-old kids how to write a letter like this?

*

I don't relate to all the fancy words they publish about every soldier who dies.

*

If this is going to be a message from another world, let it be authentic.

*

If I die by enemy hand, I want the world to hear.

*

In case I die, I'd better leave operating instructions.

*

I want you to know that there's no one happier than I am.

*

I fell with honor for the sake of my people.

I'd be very happy if they'd set something up in my memory. . .something like education.

*

Buy a good karaoke system for the gang in Dimona.

*

I'm a little scared, but I'm at peace.

*

I'm afraid that I'm a high-value target for Hamas.

*

We crawled up to here, I got injured, and there's a barrage now.

*

Dad. . .when it's all over and my friends tell you what I did here, you'll be very proud of me.

*

Suddenly, it's all clear. Our generation, our turn.

*

Now that we're done with the kitschy part, we're up to the funeral. Mom, I ask you, no tear-jerking, emotional speeches.

*

You saw how hundreds of people I don't even know came to my funeral?

*

Grandpa, I know that you always believed in me and you were very proud of me becoming a fighter. So be proud now, too, because I didn't fall in vain.

*

Every once in a while, smile up at the clouds – I'll be there.

*

If I had to sculpt my life all over again, I wouldn't change a thing.

*

I hope that you'll remember me.

***

We remember the moment we first read these words, in the throes of the October 7th War (known operationally as Swords of Iron). We had already heard so many words during this war – testimonies, stories, interviews, but from our first encounter with a soldier's last letter, we were moved in a different way. What even is this? This beauty? Who writes like this? So vulnerable, penetrating, singular, unlike anything else. As people who work with words, we were left speechless.

We were speechless both in the face of these words, and of the very choice to write. Imagine the abnormal situation of a young soldier or a middle-aged reservist making the unfathomably courageous choice to contemplate the possibility of not returning from the battlefield, and writing a last letter.

We couldn't yet articulate just why, even to ourselves, but we felt that we couldn't let these words get swept away with the usual flood of current events and news reports. We felt that they were worthy of the highest honor; they deserved to live on.

And we also thought: There must be so many more of them.

These last words are treasures. So let's collect them.

Let's create a book that compiles the last letters of soldiers that fell in this war – those that have already been published, and especially those that haven't been.

But wait, we asked ourselves – why? Why us, why now? Why should we delve so deeply into this pain, get so close to the grief of mourning? Why dive into a whole sea of texts whose common denominator is that their authors are here no more? Why look death in the eye instead of looking away?

And then we understood: That's exactly what they did, the fallen. They dared look death straight in the eye, to contemplate the possibility that they would never return, and compose these last letters.

If they had the courage to write them, then we should summon the courage to read them.

The small, blue Star of David you see on the cover was drawn by Adi Leon, of blessed memory, at the end of his last letter, which he wrote the night before he went into Gaza.

In that letter, he wrote about what he had seen on October 7th, about the dangerous battle he was about to face, and about the knowledge that he might not return. He wrote to his parents, to his little sister, and to the people of Israel. At the bottom of the page, he drew a small heart and a Star of David.

He ended the letter with the words "I hope you'll remember me."

If you are reading these words, you are helping to fulfill Adi's humble request: to remember him, and to remember the forty-eight other heroes whose final letters are collected in this book. They went out to defend the country and the people they loved so deeply.

Despite the geographical distance, this book brings you very close to this generation of soldiers – the beautiful faces of Israel in 2023. Throughout the war, we as Israelis felt the warm embrace of our people in Jewish communities all over the world, as well as the support of our non-Jewish friends and all people of good will and moral clarity, who understood what we were fighting for. We experienced our fellow Jews' tremendous willingness to help, and our shared pain.

We felt the Jewish people's great love for our soldiers.

The book you now hold in your hands is living testimony to the deep love our soldiers had for the Jewish people – in their own words.

This war touched us, and all Israelis, personally.

On October 7th Shlomo's uncle, Amram Alon Toledano of blessed memory, was murdered by Hamas terrorists in Sderot on his way to the synagogue. When we first started thinking about this book, and throughout our work on it, Racheli lived in fear for the lives of her reservist husband Nitai, her brothers in the service, and all her relatives off fighting in Gaza and Lebanon. Every day at work as a journalist, she kept in touch with bereaved families. The boundaries between the personal and the national, the individual and the collective, broke down.

A single day shattered the border between life and death. Death beckoned to us from bumper stickers in the street; from social gatherings; from official death notices. And we cannot look away any longer. Nor should we want to.

How This Book Was Created

We weren't quite sure how to create a book like this, so we decided to get started and learn as we went along. We understood that the letters that made it into the news were a fraction of what was out there, and that we didn't want to let a single one of these treasures slip away, its letters floating off into the air.

We thought about posting a public appeal in newspapers and social media, but we felt that reaching out to each bereaved family personally would be a more sensitive and appropriate way to invite them to share something so precious. So we started working systematically: We made an Excel sheet of all the fallen soldiers.

We found the families' contact information through every acquaintance, organization, and commemoration project we could think of, and slowly, we amassed many, many phone numbers. And with each new official death notice, we brokenheartedly added another name to the spreadsheet, which was already far too long.

We began reaching out to the families of all the soldiers who fell in the first year of the war. We soon realized that we wouldn't manage to get hold of all the hundreds of families by ourselves, so we looked for researchers to organize the effort. We were concerned that the process would become too technical. We wanted to keep it as personal and intimate as we could, so we sought professionals with a rare combination of sensitivity, thoroughness, and warmth. And we found Aviv Baavur and Tehila Ben Harush, who were all this and more.

Aviv and Tehila worked around the clock for months to contact each family, explain the project, embrace them and invite them to join. They went back and forth with us about each complex dilemma – for example, whether to approach the parents of the surveillance soldiers who were killed on October 7th, where the chances that a letter had been left were infinitesimal, or to risk overlooking them.

Aviv and Tehila, thank you for your devotion and your big hearts. It was a privilege to work with you.

We did our best to reach out to each family, and if we missed anyone, we ask their forgiveness.

Soon after we began reaching out to the families, it became clear that the overwhelming majority of soldiers did not leave a last letter. There is no formal IDF guideline encouraging soldiers to write letters before going out to battle; soldiers who write do so on their own initiative.

Some families shared their aching sense of loss at missing out on words their sons never got to write. Others were relieved that their loved ones fought without thought of death.

Some parents said that they had a letter, but were reluctant to share one of the most precious, intimate things they had left from their sons. Even so, many of them ultimately made the magnanimous choice to share the letters, so that these last words might comfort others as they themselves had been comforted.

Most of the letters in this book have never been published before. When we approached families whose son's letters had already been published, we almost always discovered that only one page or section of a longer letter had been made public – usually the paragraph beginning with something like "If I die." The families assumed that the more personal parts of the letters would be less interesting to others. We thought the opposite – that these were the most engaging and individual parts of the letters; fortunately, our enthusiasm proved to be contagious.

"I'm not sure he would have wanted us to share this," one of the fathers said to us, "but you know what? If he has a problem with it, let him come and say so."

We received hundreds of exquisite texts, but we had to narrow them down. We set a very specific criterion: The book was to consist only of letters written as last letters, letters written in the "If you're reading this, it means..." mindset. Therefore, excerpts from journals or letters sent to family and friends that only became last words in retrospect were not included in this book. This meant that we had to regretfully turn down several beautiful texts that didn't fit this concept.

We were left with dozens of letters, all very different, with one thing in common: All were written with the knowledge that they would be read only if the author was no longer with us.

When we studied these words, we felt that we were holding a piece of history. And we knew that was how we must present them – without any filters, without correcting words or commas, even if the spelling was off or the phrasing was a little awkward, because these were not our own. We remained fiercely faithful to the originals, to the raw material. We didn't censor a single word – we only omitted words that the family chose to withhold for the sake of privacy or those that were destroyed because the paper was burnt or damaged.

After months of gathering materials, we were left with forty-nine last letters.

And then we understood that that was only the beginning.

We realized that none of the letters was written in a vacuum. Each letter has a story. Some soldiers wrote on October 7th during a brief respite between fierce battles in the Gaza Envelope. Others wrote just before their phones were collected by the army in preparation for entering Gaza, when they sensed that it was their last chance to write.

Some soldiers wrote in notepads in the heart of Rafah, after losing close friends. One wrote before embarking on a mission to rescue hostages; he said he was well aware of the danger involved and prepared to pay the price.

There were also many who didn't write any letters over long months of fighting, only to decide to write mere days or even hours before they fell in battle – as if they somehow knew.

The story of how each letter was written became an integral part of this book. We clarified and researched as much background information as we could. This became the introduction to each letter: When did he decide to write? Where was he, and what was he going through at that time? Whom did he tell about the letter? How did he keep it from being read before he fell?

Often, even the family didn't know the full story, so we spoke with the friends, the commanders, the officers who kept the letters safe – with anyone who might be able to fill in another piece of the puzzle. We were motivated to gather and document as much concrete information as possible; to create a time capsule for future generations.

We read each letter again and again, meditating on each one, and the questions just kept coming. How could it be that Yoav, mortally wounded, wrote that it was "the best twenty minutes of my life"? Alon requested that a brewery be established in his memory. What happened in the end with that? What was Yonatan talking about when he wrote, "The images that I saw are stuck in my head – I'm going out to battle for their sake"? How could Elchanan Kalmanson – who fell at the very beginning of the surprise attack, on October 8 – manage to write a last letter? And what is that little sketch of a cat that Adi drew in the middle of his?

We also lingered over what might seem like small, marginal details. We stopped at every phrase that seemed to echo a private joke, refer to the tail end of a story, or leave the vaguest hint. We allowed our curiosity to lead the way, and this stage of the work became part investigation, part literary analysis. We tried to read between the lines and get a sense of the person behind them, who put his heart into them.

We so badly wanted to talk to the writers themselves; to sit with them over a cup of coffee and ask them everything. If we only could. Instead, in lieu of the letter writers, we turned to their addressees – their parents, partners, and friends.

It was important to us to meet with each family personally and directly, without mediation. To look them in the eye and read their loved one's last letter together with them, word by word. This was one of the most emotional stages of creating this book – looking at it together with them, watching as many of the parents saw the letter through a new set of eyes in conversation with us, reading it anew and uncovering aspects they hadn't noticed before. One of the mothers stopped us in the middle and asked, through tears, "Wait, you read all of the letters like this, interpreting each and every word as if it were a sacred text?"

And we answered, "What do you mean, 'as if'?"

Deep connections were forged by our shared study of each letter. Forty-nine families made their way into our hearts, and there they remain. Thank you for entrusting us with this privilege. We did our best to be worthy of the mission.

Throughout the reading process, we felt again and again that the letters were so intimate that it was almost wrong to read them, like taking a peek into someone's diary. In many cases, we actually were peeking into someone's diary without permission, reading the final words that a person wrote himself. For this reason, the families became our moral compass; we asked their consent for each word we added about their sons in the introductions to the letters and the notes.

We had to show great restraint. Long hours of conversation with soldiers' families and friends were condensed into the brief notes at the bottom of each letter. We chose to write in a minimalist style. To use few adjectives or superlatives. To let the facts speak for themselves. We also took care not to embellish or sugarcoat what we learned. The truth is beautiful as is.

We were often tempted to add another detail about his music, her dreams, to describe their heroic last battle. But we reminded ourselves that this book isn't the story of our heroes' lives or even of their deaths, but the story of their last letters. And that not everything needs to be said.

Leave the Rest
Shlomo Tanny
Don't say it all.
Even a tree says only trunk and leaves,
And leaves roots in the darkness.
Don't cross all the boundaries.
Even God tells only of sun,
Moon and stars,
And leaves universes
Beyond the griefs of knowledge.
Don't read a man all the way to the end.

These last letters were written in every format imaginable – by hand, on WhatsApp, on the computer, a voice note, a video clip. For the sake of consistency, we decided to transcribe each letter, word for word, and that they would all appear in the same font.

This was a difficult decision. Handwriting is fiercely intimate; we didn't want to give that up. We wanted to present the letters in all their rawness – the charred paper, the trembling hand, to give expression to the original, to the handwriting itself. And then we had the idea of turning to Ot.Hayim, "Living Letters." Ot.Hayim is a beautiful volunteer memorial initiative started in the midst of this war, in which graphic designers work in conjunction with bereaved families to create fonts out of the handwriting of the fallen, to memorialize their names and individuality. The Ot.Hayim volunteers used the handwriting of the heroes of this book as a basis to sensitively, lovingly recreate the final words of the last letters in the book. We are truly grateful.

***

The intense encounter with all these last letters and the constant proximity to grief and death and longing flooded us with feelings and questions. We felt that we were confronting something bigger than us, and we didn't want to face it alone. We asked ourselves whom we'd want to guide us – and future readers – as we read through these words.

We assembled a group of inspiring figures from the world of Israeli culture – people of insight and heart. We talked with them and asked them to write words of their own about these last words.

These creators read the letters in this book and then donated their words and intimate thoughts. We were expecting meaningful philosophical and literary reflections, but they gave us far more: their heart, their vulnerability, their very selves. Each wrote from their own perspective and life experience, and together their reflections form an exquisite Israeli symposium on last words.

Thank you, President Isaac Herzog, Eviatar Banai, Rabbanit Yemima Mizrachi, Rabbi Tamir Granot, Lieutenant Colonel Aviran Alfasi, Emily Damari, Iris Haim, Avi Issacharoff, and Miriam Peretz. Thank you for your dialogue, for thinking along with us, and for agreeing to open your hearts. Thank you for bearing this burden together with us.

Thank you to the true authors of this book, who will never read it. We fell in love with you even though we never met. How you wished that no one would have to read these words. Thank you for choosing to write and to leave something of yourselves for all of us – inspiring us to live and love more than before.

As we worked with your last words, we repeatedly asked ourselves what you would think of this book. Some of you would definitely have laughed at us for being too kitschy. "I don't relate to all the fancy words."

"Be doers, not talkers." But what can we do – your words are truly great and precious to us. We won't let go of them.

We don't really know how to thank people who sacrificed their lives for our sake. But for starters, we're here, looking right at you and reading your words.

Over the course of working on this book, people sometimes asked us: Wait, who do you actually work for? Are you part of some kind of organization or commemorative branch of government?

And sometimes we asked ourselves, when it was hard, what we had to do with all this. We're in truth not part of any official group or organization; we're just two people, a copywriter and a journalist; no one appointed us or commissioned us to take on this project.

And each time we hesitated or wavered, the words of six-year-old Romi Suissa from Sderot – who was hiding in the back seat with her three-year-old sister when terrorists murdered her parents in their car – resonated for us. When rescuers came to the car, Romi asked them, "Are you with Israel?"

And this is our answer: We are with Israel. That's what we're a part of.

We Israelis have never in our lifetimes been brought as low as we were on October 7th. Yet also in our lifetimes, we have never felt as proud to be sons and daughters of Israel. Throughout this difficult war, a spirit of voluntarism has swept the country, everyone doing their part.

We are people of words, so we have gathered this bouquet of words for our people. We lay it here before you.

Now it is yours.

Shlomo Kavas and Racheli Palant-Rozen
25 Shevat 5785/26 February 2025
Day 509 of the October 7th War

Foreword

President Isaac Herzog

Days of harsh warfare have come upon us, beginning with the biggest, most terrible, horrific, and savage massacre that we have experienced since our return to our land; even now, over a year since that bitter and fateful day, we are scarred, shocked, and overwhelmed. We are still far from processing, understanding, and putting into words the painful burden we have borne since October 7th, Simchat Torah.

Throughout this time period, we have all of us veered between anxiety and hope, pain and faith, in an impossible conjunction of life and death, grief and love, longing and intense agony. And in an astonishing way, though our shoulders bend under the weight of our sadness, we hold our backs more straight – buoyed by the privilege of being part of this people, that these are our sons and daughters.

Every day more stories of the courage, audacity, and nobility of our brave soldiers and citizens come to our attention. Male and female fighters who did not wait around for orders; who girded themselves for battle and charged into fire; citizens, men and women, who, with a breathtaking statement of "Here I am," risked their lives instead of standing by, even on that cursed day when the enemy broke into homes and, with monstrous, merciless cruelty, burned and slaughtered mothers and children, the young and the old, seekers of peace. They came because their hearts called them to action, and they stood guard with strength and might that cannot be surpassed. Soldiers who have continued to fight, for months on end, some of them parents, some of them just engaged, some of them new recruits, putting their lives on hold to protect their people. They have gone out to the bloody, cruel battlefields of Gaza, Judea, Samaria, and Lebanon to bring back our safety, our security, and our brothers and sisters tortured and held hostage by the terrorists of Hamas. For all its horrors, this war has revealed to us the full glory and splendor of our shining warriors. For the sake of our people, so that good and light will prevail, they have given their lives with a sense of purpose, with love for nation and homeland, with their eyes open and hearts awake.

Compiling their last letters – written before going out to battles from which they did not return – is a most precious, powerful, and worthy task. These letters – in all their beauty and lucidity, the clear and comprehending gaze that peeks out from behind them – must become part of our people's eternal heritage, with all the trembling and turmoil that sometimes come across, and maybe because of them. They are Holy Writ, letters rising from parchment that went up in flame, insofar as they bear tidings, and faith and a binding command: to continue life here, to do great good, and – together, shoulder to shoulder – to deepen our hold on our only home, the home for whose existence so many wondrous people have fallen. To reaffirm our commitment to the Eternal of Israel and to Israel's unity, in a home that must be perfected, whole, strong, and worthy of the immense sacrifice our beautiful, beloved, and courageous sons and daughters have made for its sake.

> *Know that time and enemies, wind and water, shall not erase you:*
> *you shall go on, made of letters.*
> Haim Gouri

May we be worthy of them and their letters,
In blessing and with deep appreciation,
Isaac Herzog
President of Israel

Letters

Eden Provisor

Captain Eden Provisor, from Alfei Menashe, tank officer in the 52nd Battalion, 401st (Armored) Brigade. He fell in combat in the Gaza Strip on 5 Kislev 5784/ November 18, 2023. He is survived by his parents and three siblings. He was twenty-one when he fell.

Eden was chosen to command the brigade's lead tank, from the first day of the ground campaign in Gaza until he fell.

On November 15, 2023, he called his family from Gaza with a cell phone belonging to a noncommissioned officer bringing supplies to the field.

After long conversations with his mother and siblings, he asked his father to stay on the line by himself.

Eden didn't have time to write during the intense fighting, so he told his father, Guy, "Dad, now I'm dictating my last words to you."

His father wrote the words down and held onto them.

Three days later, Eden fell in battle, and his father first shared Eden's last words with the rest of the family.

When It's All Over, You'll Be Very Proud of Me

Eden Provisor

Dad, I want to speak with you, seriously, and ***I'm asking you to listen to me without getting angry at me.***

Dad, ***we're here in the inferno*** *and the situation is terrible. I can't tell you what will happen, but* ***there's a chance that I won't be coming back home,*** *but will be staying here. I'm asking you to listen to me: I want you to continue living as if I'm with you.*

Don't collapse and don't live in sadness. I'm asking you to continue to enjoy life, to go out to restaurants and travel abroad

I'm asking you to listen to me without getting angry at me: When Eden left for battle, his father, Guy, handed him a letter with two requests: to bring all his soldiers safely back home, and not to do anything that would earn him a commendation. Eden's soldiers told them that before they went into Gaza, he read them his father's letter and cried. He knew that he wouldn't be able to fulfill his father's requests.

We're here in the inferno: As Eden's battalion advanced, more and more anti-tank missiles were fired at them. Eden, who was the commander of the lead tank, knew that he was an especially vulnerable target. Two days after his conversation with his father, during their attack on Jabaliya, Eden's tank took a direct missile hit, and Eden was killed.

There's a chance that I won't be coming back home: The day after that conversation, Eden's father called him and asked him to take back those parting words – or to come right back home. "I asked him to find someone to take his place. That was the first time that Eden ever shouted at me. He said: 'That's not an option. You raised me for this – for leadership, for responsibility. This is the role that they gave me. If someone takes my place and gets hurt instead of me, I won't be able to live with it, not for a single day.'"

and all the things we loved to do. Dad, I'm serious; you can't do anything else. I want you to know that I'm proud of what I'm doing, and even if something happens to me then it'll happen, and it's all right. I'm on my life's mission, watching over the Land of Israel.

When it's all over and my friends tell you what I did here, you'll be very proud of me. *You gave me everything in life and I ask that you really listen to me.*

I had a good life, a full life, full of happiness and goodness. I hope that God will be with me, but even if not – you should all know that I loved you and I had a terrific life.

Dad, you have to promise me this, because that's the only way I can go on.

אבא אתה חייב להבטיח לי את זה
כי רק ככה אני יכול להמשיך.

When it's all over and my friends tell you what I did here, you'll be very proud of me: After his death, Eden's friends told his family stories of his courage.

One story is that as they entered the Al-Shati Camp, Eden's battalion was ambushed by dozens of anti-tank missiles. When there was finally a lull after hours of fierce battle, the battalion commander updated their force about a high-ranking Hamas commander in the area who was about to escape.

Radio silence. After the intense fight, no one was in a hurry to return to the line of fire.

After a few moments of tense silence, Eden's voice echoed over the radio: "Commander, this is Three. We're going out to attack."

In a separate incident, Eden's tank was malfunctioning, so they moved out of the range of fire. As they were waiting, a few kilometers away from the battlefield, Eden noticed that a certain officer wasn't responding on the radio and he became worried about him. He rushed his crew back into the malfunctioning tank, which he miraculously managed to start, and on his own initiative, drove back into the heart of the battle. "A friend is trapped, and we all have to save him," he said to his soldiers. When they reached the officer, they discovered that he was wounded and unconscious, and they saved his life.

Yoav Malayev

Lieutenant Yoav Malayev, from Kiryat Ono, deputy battalion communications officer in the 77th Battalion, 7th (Armored) Brigade. He fell in combat at the Yiftaḥ outpost on 22 Tishrei 5784/ October 7th, 2023. He is survived by his parents, three siblings, and a partner. He was nineteen when he fell.

From basic training until his final moments, Yoav kept a small pocket journal. Inside its back cover was a page that Yoav had torn out of the pad. He'd written across the top: "Take a look when it gets tough." Under the title he had written: "Head held high. Set an example. Be the best. Pursue contact. Reset and switch mindsets. Go all out."

On October 7th Yoav led a fierce battle against Hamas terrorists who were trying to invade the Yiftaḥ outpost next to Zikim.

After about an hour of tenacious fighting he was mortally wounded. In the few brief minutes between his injury and his death, Yoav chose to use the last of his strength to fish out his notepad, even though he also had his cell phone on him. He wrote down his last words in weak, blurred handwriting.

The Best Twenty Minutes of My Life

Yoav Malayev

The best twenty minutes of my life.

We crawled up to here, I got injured, and there's a barrage now.

I'm thinking of you and will be thinking of you the whole journey,

I love you.

The best twenty minutes of my life: "In order to understand Yoav's brief, astounding sentence," his parents Maya and Alex explain, "you have to delve into everything that was encapsulated into those minutes, which were the essence of everything Yoav reminded himself of in the 'Take a look when it's hard' note."

Due to a medical issue, Yoav could have been exempt from combat service, but he fought for it, and managed to become a combat track teleprocessing officer.

During the days leading up to October 7th, Yoav decided on his own initiative, out of a sense of responsibility for his battalion's readiness for combat, to devote whole nights to fixing – alongside another soldier – all the communications malfunctions of all the tanks in that sector, which was very quiet at the time.

On October 6, in response to a WhatsApp message from his father asking how he was, Yoav wrote: "I'm doing as well as my tanks are – not great."

On the morning of October 7th, when the missiles started falling, Yoav managed to help that other soldier, who was gripped with anxiety. He hugged her and told her, "I want you to always remember that, thanks to you, there are now four more working tanks at the border fence."

Yoav was the officer on duty, and despite his lack of combat experience, he took charge of the fighting at the outpost.

He instructed the armed soldiers in the shelter to stay and protect the unarmed soldiers inside instead of following him. Then, with five other soldiers, he ran to hold back the hordes of terrorists who were lying in ambush at the base's gate.

In the first and last battle of his life, Yoav encouraged and supported the more experienced combat soldiers who fought at his side and together, outnumbered, they succeeded in preventing the outpost from being overthrown.

I love you: Yoav, who chose his words carefully throughout his life, didn't specify to whom these words were addressed. "He chose exactly what to write and didn't omit a word," his parents say. "He wrote to everyone who loved him – and a lot of people loved him." They are comforted by the knowledge that his last words were words of love.

Alon Sacagiu

Captain Alon Sacagiu, from Hadera, enlisted into the Duvdevan Counter-Terror Unit, Commando Brigade, and after an officer's course, became commander of the sniper team in the Haruv Commando Unit, Kfir Brigade. He fell in combat during an operation in the Jenin Refugee Camp on 21 Sivan 5784/June 27, 2024. He is survived by his parents, sister, brother, and girlfriend. He was twenty-two when he fell.

Alon wrote this letter on November 22, 2023, before entering Gaza, in a password-protected note in the Notes app on his phone entitled "In case that."

He told his friend Ido about the letter and gave him the password. Ido also wrote a goodbye letter, on paper. They agreed that when they came out of Gaza, they would destroy the letters together. Both made it out safely. Ido burned his letter, but Alon didn't delete his.

After participating in many missions in Gaza, Alon went on to operations in Judea and Samaria. During a battle in Jenin, as he was evacuating wounded soldiers under fire, an explosive was detonated on Alon and his soldiers. Alon's body absorbed most of the explosive shock and he was killed. All twenty or so soldiers that were around him were saved.

During the shiva, Alon's family received his cell phone, which was shattered by the explosion. They managed to read his last letter through the shards of the screen.

I Don't Relate to All the Fancy Words They Publish

Alon Sacagiu

In case that

I want you ***to set up a brewery in my memory that you'll call "Duvdevan"*** *with a few kinds of beer to be developed over time, as follows:*

Bli Wassah – "No showing off"; an amber beer similar to Goldstar

Ragua – "Chill"; wheat beer

"IPA" – Just an India Pale Ale

"90" – A 9-percent-alcohol beer, very strong and tasty

"Panther"— Beer that everyone loves that works for everyone

"It's a Dream" – A special dark beer/duvdevan cherry beer

Meduyeket – "Hits the Spot"; a beer with a taste reminiscent of Weihenstephan that simply hits the spot (like a sniper 😉)

To set up a brewery in my memory that you'll call "Duvdevan": Every Friday Alon and his friends would hang out together with their partners at the same brewery.

Duvdevan: The name of Alon's army unit.

Since Alon was killed, his friends have been busy fulfilling his ambitious request. Sharon, his partner, who doesn't personally like beer, runs the Instagram @duvdevan_beer, documenting the process of establishing the brewery in Alon's memory.

Goldstar, was also touched by Alon's last words, and produced a special-edition beer in his memory with Alon's name and excerpts of his last letter printed on the label.

*Twenty to 30 percent of company profits will be donated to "**the unit that's a dream.**" You can play around with the names; I approve.*

Once a year, a brewery event, good meat (hamburgers/grill), stalls, a good coffee cart, and lots of beer. The event should be in honor of the unit, in my name – nothing too crowded, modest with a lot of happy people.

***At my funeral, I want them to play the song "Beautiful Things to See"** by **Idan Amedi** – listen to the words, and move on; "there are more beautiful things to see..."*

*I don't relate to all the fancy words they publish about every soldier who dies, writing as if they're **Alterman,** at the very least.*

I believe in deeds and putting things into action and I believe that I did everything I could to protect the people and the place that I love the most. Be doers, not talkers.

The unit that's a dream: An Israeli catchphrase for elite army units.

At my funeral I want you to play the song "Beautiful Things to See": This wish wasn't yet known at the time of the funeral, since Alon's family only received his phone with the last letter during the week of shiva. Instead, Omri Glickman, a soloist from the Israeli band "HaTikvah 6," sang "BaOlam Shelah" (In Her World), the song Alon and Sharon had planned to play as they walked down the aisle at their wedding.

A few days after Alon's family read the letter, Israeli singer Idan Amedi went to visit them and sang this song. "I've sung a lot of songs at funerals," Idan said, "but they've never asked me to sing such an optimistic song before."

The song's refrain:
My love, stop seeing the end.
My love, this it would seem is what had to be.
That's what you say.
Come let's keep living; there are more beautiful things to see.

Idan Amedi: Israeli singer and actor who was himself injured in the war during reserve duty.

Alterman: The renowned Israeli poet Nathan Alterman, 1910–1970.

Mom and Dad

I don't have much to write to you. I hope that you know what I think of you.

I love you so much and thank you for everything you've done for me my whole life; you raised me great. Thank you for not letting up on me; you pushed and you were there at the tough moments.

Don't be sad, keep on living and smiling for the family; be good people. I love you lots.

Amit

I wish you success in everything you do, that you'll find a good, quality guy, marry him and make yourself a warm, loving family. Take life easy and smile, it'll do you good.

Ariel

I don't know how well you'll remember me, but continue on my path, be a good person, help, volunteer, and succeed. You're an amazing kid. Have good values and love our country, protect it and push yourself to the max.

I'm sure you'll reach much higher places than I did.

I request – without too many posts and interviews and nonsense, you can talk or tell stories but not too much, no interviews with the uncle who goes on about how good and amazing he was.... I don't like that nonsense.

Sharon

I love you. Thank you for each happy moment, every hug, every kiss, all your help, every moment of quiet you gave me. Thank you for being there for me come fire or water.

I'm not able to imagine myself without you. It's just so different; you're part of my life.

I saw us getting married and bringing beautiful kids into the world and it was all planned out in my head; unfortunately we won't get to have that, but you need to keep going.

Don't let this get you depressed or ***thinking that you'll lose everyone close to you****; smile! Keep living, do good around you, remember me and move forward, start a family and love them more than you loved me.*

You're the best thing that ever happened to me and my wish is that things will be good for you. I'm looking down and watching over you always.

I ask of you – no drama and unnecessary posts, no need to make ***the standard girlfriend post****.*

Find your own way to remember/remind others.

Thinking that you'll lose everyone close to you: Sharon's father was killed in a workplace accident when she was four years old. Her brother lost his partner at the Nova Music Festival massacre on October 7th. Alon, who knew how many loved ones she'd lost, tried to give her strength in case she would lose him as well.

The standard girlfriend post: Sharon and Alon would talk about everything, and laughed sometimes about death as well. Alon would show her social media posts by partners of fallen soldiers and tease her: "If something happens to me, will you write like that, too?"

Friends

If you're reading this letter and don't succeed in forming a clear view of what I think of you, then I've failed. I love each and every one of you; it felt superfluous to write separately to each of you.

You made my life better and fuller and I thank you for that. I love all of you and I'll be watching over you from above with pride knowing that you're all going on with your lives thanks to me, and no one is happier than I am.

Smile, be good people, give of yourselves to our country, and live with no regrets.

Always remember: no question marks, just exclamation points!

You have tasks to continue from me. I hope that everyone knows what they are, and whoever doesn't – I'll come tell him in a dream or ***through my grandma****.*

Through my grandma: Alon's grandmother reads coffee grinds and tarot cards. When Alon and his friends would go home, they would hop over to see her for a reading and advice. Alon is promising his friends that if they don't complete the tasks he expects of them, he'll remind them through her.

Team 90

Team 90, you're one of the best things that happened to me in my life. Thank you for all the experiences that you gave me and all the amazing moments I had with you. I love each and every one of you; keep living and doing good for the country. Be a part of our unit and its ***non-profit foundation.***

There are no words that could explain how much love I have for the team; remember me and live the life I didn't get to.

I fought for Itay and for Orush and Ben and Gedalia and everyone who left us along the way.

Non-profit foundation: It is common for Israelis after military service to continue to get together and support their units through associated non-profits.

I fought for Itay and Orush and Ben and Gedalia and everyone who left us along the way:
After his death, the family found a locked note on Alon's phone entitled "For Their Sake." The note is a list of names, dates of death or burial (all in 2023), and cemeteries:
Itay Yehuda Bausi – 10/12 Kevutzat Yavneh
Liav Alush – 12/17 Gedera Cemetery
Ben Bronstein – 10/11 Holon Cemetery
Or (Orush) Yosef Ran – 10/10 Gevaot Olam
Pedaya Mark – 11/1 Har HaMenuhot [a large cemetery in Jerusalem].
Yosef Guedalia – 10/11 Har Herzl [a military cemetery in Jerusalem]
Yuval Yafeh – 10/13 Tzofit Cemetery
Ben Shelly – 12/14 Kidron
When Alon got leave from the army, before he went home, he would visit his friends in the cemetery.

Sniper Team

You're in my heart, each and every one of you.

I did everything I could to prepare you for this day, this moment.

Now is the time for results. If you're reading this I guess you'll have to go on without me.

I hope that I succeeded in creating the team that we dreamed of and aspired to, to create an aura of respect and appreciation around the snipers and around the team.

Carry on my mission and never give up, no matter how many times they try to stop you.

Whoever doesn't swim drowns, especially in Haruv…

I was privileged to meet amazing people with a lot of willpower and ability.

You gave me the privilege of being your commander and leading you in battle. You believed in me and followed my lead.

Keep learning and improving; strive to achieve skills and love what you do.

The situation has brought up a lot of thoughts and points of emphasis for me, but I won't get to implement them. I hope that you've come up with things for yourselves and that you get to put them into practice.

Stay fierce, and take care of yourselves.

I love and appreciate you.

אוהב אותכם ומעריך.

Elchanan Kalmanson

Major (Reserves) Elchanan Meir Kalmanson, from Otniel, Mossad man and IDF officer in the Judea and Samaria Division Command, Border Defense Corps. He fell in the battle over Kibbutz Be'eri on 23 Tishrei 5784/ October 8, 2023. He is survived by his wife, five children, parents, and five siblings. He was forty-two when he fell.

Elchanan worked for the Mossad and lived in danger for many years. Long before the war, he decided to save a last letter on his personal computer, rewriting and updating it over the years. He last updated it after Yom HaZikaron, Israel's Memorial Day, in 2023. Elchanan told no one about the letter.

On October 7th, Elchanan rushed out of his home in Otniel on his own initiative, before receiving any orders, and drove out to defend the Gaza Envelope. He led an ad hoc group made up of his brother and nephew, nicknamed "Team Elchanan." They fought in Kibbutz Be'eri and rescued about a hundred residents. After sixteen straight hours of fighting, Elchanan fell in combat.

After his death, Elchanan's wife, Shlomit, found a file on his computer entitled "If I Die." The letter had been right there for years, not even password protected, but Shlomit didn't notice it until that day.

Parts of the letter are excerpted here.

I Want the World to Hear

Elchanan Kalmanson

If I die by enemy hand, ***I want the world to hear****.*

No one should avenge or call for revenge. Whoever I take out with me (I hope) – I'll take out.

Whoever feels such burning in their bones – let them burn with life. [...]

In the event that our people do not regain their sanity and decide one day to evacuate Otniel as well, I ask that they not clear out or move ***my grave****. Don't pour cement and don't hide it. Leave me in place, in the place where I lived.*

If our enemies decide to destroy/pillage/wreck/plow over, let me at least be there to show their true nature.

[...] I believed in the path. I believed in the return of our people to our land. ***I believed in the small deed that makes a great difference.*** *A little detail that can save lives.*

I want the world to hear: The world heard. On Yom HaAtzma'ut, Israeli Independence Day, in 2024, "Team Elchanan" was awarded the Israel Prize for Civil Courage. The Department of Education added a unit of study to the national school curriculum that includes their story. Elchanan Kalmanson became one of the best-known symbols of heroism on October 7th.

My grave: Elchanan Kalmanson's grave is the only grave in Israel that is engraved with both the insignia of the IDF and the insignia of the Mossad.

I believed in the small deed that makes a great difference: On October 7th, Team Elchanan went from home to home in Kibbutz Be'eri, rescuing its residents under heavy fire. In between bouts of combat, they learned of an old woman who was hard of hearing and

[...] If I fall as a casualty in a war over the land – let them remember and bring back to mind that this isn't another war or another intifada or some other nonsense. This is the same long war over our country and our people's identity that's already been going on for nearly 150 years.

I wanted and I tried to be a person, to be a Jew.

רציתי וניסיתי להיות אדם, להיות יהודי

needed rescuing. Before Elchanan went inside her home, his brother Menachem made it clear to him that they had no time to spare: "No hearing aids, no medication. Everything can be bought. You go in, get her, and bring her out."

Nevertheless, Elchanan did take a few minutes to get the woman's medication and hearing aids before bringing her out. Menachem was angry, but Elchanan explained: "We must not let these people escape from their homes like refugees. We have to pay attention not just to getting them out, but also to how we get them out. They have to exit their homes like people, heads held high."

I wanted and I tried to be a person, to be a Jew: When Team Elchanan came to rescue the residents of one home in Be'eri, the terrified family refused to open their shelter door. They were afraid that terrorists were knocking at the door, pretending to be Israelis. Elchanan and his team introduced themselves by name and spoke to them in Hebrew from outside the door, but they still couldn't convince the family to believe them. Only after they shouted out the *Shema* prayer, "Hear O Israel, the Lord is our God, the Lord is One," did the family open the door.

Ori Nechemya Ashkenazi

Sergeant Ori Nechemya Ashkenazi, from Ashkelon, served in the 46th Battalion, 401st (Armored) Brigade. He fell in combat in the southern Gaza Strip on 18 Av 5784/August 22, 2024. He is survived by his parents, two siblings, and a partner. He was nineteen when he fell.

Ori wrote his last letter on April 18, 2024, as he was undergoing combat training. He saved it in his phone's Notes app, entitled, "In the event that…"

After his first stint in Rafah, Ori told his older brother, Shalev: "You're the only one I trust to be strong enough to keep my last words for me. I have a last letter saved on my phone in Notes; you're the only one I want to know that it exists." Shalev immediately silenced him, but didn't forget the conversation.

When Shalev was notified of Ori's death, the first thing he did was to ask the IDF to get hold of Ori's phone as soon as possible.

The IDF usually gave the deceased's phone to the family together with the rest of their belongings during the week of shiva following the funeral, or soon after. But the family's casualty officer understood their pressing need to read Ori's last letter, and drove that very night to retrieve the phone from the assembly area. The family was able to read his last letter – which included instructions for his funeral – before the funeral.

Ori's last letter was instrumental in the IDF Casualty Department making it a high priority to get a fallen soldier's phone to a bereaved family as soon as possible, even before the rest of the soldier's belongings.

In the IDF minutes documenting the change in policy regarding soldiers' letters, the updated policy is referred to as the "Ori Protocol."

No Tear-Jerking, Emotional Speeches

Ori Ashkenazi Nechemya

In the Event That…

Dear family,

If you're reading this, it's reasonable to assume that things didn't go as planned, and I messed up and failed.

I don't know how to write this letter and why I'm doing this, but in the event that, I wanted there to be something you could keep, that I'd leave for you. I lived a wonderful life with no regrets with the most amazing family and partner there are. In any case let's get to the gist of it: I love you so much and I'm sorry if I caused you pain. I did what I did and this service out of utter love for this strange country of ours, and if I saved and sanctified human life when I departed then I regret nothing and ***I succeeded and failed at my mission at the same time.***

Mom and Dad – Thank you for everything and for what you did for me for my sake throughout my life and I always appreciated it even if I didn't show it. To see you happy and content brings me eternal satisfaction.

Shalev and Tohar – Keep going and have successful lives; you're so special and smart individually that I have no doubt you'll go far and make me proud, and don't forget that I'm watching over you from on high, yeah?

The extended family – Thank you for Sabbaths and memories that I'll never forget, for laughter and a smile that

I succeeded and failed at my mission at the same time: In his private notebook, he wrote under the title "My Why" – "*To protect the citizens of the State of Israel and keep them safe, to win the next war, to fight for the country,* ***to live***" [emphasis original].

never fades, a special thank-you to Grandma and Grandpa, who helped raise me and went above and beyond for me and for all the grandchildren in the family.

Shir, my teddy bear – The first thing I want to say to you is thank you for making me grow up and teaching me what first love is and for a time that I'll keep close to me forever, for a lot of special beautiful moments and memories. I love you forever.

Now that we're done with the kitschy part we're up to the funeral. Mom, I ask you – no tear-jerking emotional speeches; don't be embarrassing. I'd be happy for the [Israeli pop singer] Roni Daloomi song "Send Him Off" to be played, and ***I'd be happy if she would come sing it****. I think it suits the occasion.*

There aren't many requests, mostly that you keep my room as it is and don't turn it into a music room ***(ahem, Dad)***

Love you forever and I'll watch over you from on high. Ori

Oh, and I almost forgot the most important part: I'd be happy if you would keep me going.

Yes Mom, I was serious when I spoke with you about it.

כן אמא הייתי רציני כשדיברתי איתך על זה

I'd be happy if she would come sing it: Roni Daloomi was abroad at the time of Ori's death and couldn't get back in time. She came to Ori's memorial service a month after his death and sang the song that he requested:
Send him off, let him go free,
Though you know that he'll never return to you.
Send him off, let him go home,
To the sheaves that sway in the breeze.

Ahem, Dad: David, Ori's father, plays the electric guitar, and was always looking for somewhere to store all his amplifiers and instruments, which became a family joke whenever space freed up in the house. As per Ori's request, his room remains exactly as it was.

If We're Scared, We Won't Be Worthy of Them

Eviatar Banai, musician, singer, and songwriter

A few years ago, I had a conversation with a teenage cancer patient in his final days, a mysterious conversation that's seared into my mind.

I asked him what he sees when his eyes are closed. Is he able to see expanses within himself?

He said that he sees giant waterfalls, like Niagara Falls in Canada. "There are marvelous sights within me. Landscapes and waterfalls. There's a world within me." That's what he said. "I'm ready to behold the wonder of the very end. Death and eternity, body and soul, pain and beauty, it's all mixed up together inside me." That's what he said.

We understood each other, and were moved to have found a friend. He was the first – perhaps the only – person I've met who was willing to see beauty within the bitter and cruel truth of being taken away.

The last letters of young people, marching with unfathomable courage into the inferno. The rage this provokes at God, and at the state and its leaders. The fear of emptiness and despair. It's impossible to read a book like this.

So very sad, heartrending. Crushing. Frightening.

But the thing is, the fear and refusal to contemplate this are more dangerous than the terrible pain of consenting to read on.

Rage and fear, as I see it, are far more dangerous than reading and weeping, and weeping; than facing the emptiness and doubt, and releasing them through tears and communion.

In the nineties movie *American Beauty* there's a poetic character, a teenager who films his life. Everything. He sees wonder and beauty in all things and the camera is his paintbrush for capturing the wonder. He films a paper bag fluttering in the autumn breeze, he films his father hitting him, he films the girl from the house across the street, and he even films a homeless woman dying in the street from an overdose. He's open to everything that this life has to offer: light and darkness, pain and rage, lust and violence. He has no fear. He films and captures it all. Pain turns into poetry when we consent to it, when we don't harden our hearts.

Don't close off your heart. That will make everything colder and more dangerous. The courage and the beauty of these young people, the price that their families paid, all that unending beauty – bound up with a vast, cruel, and unfathomable pain – seeks a home inside our hearts.

It seeks to change us.

If we get scared and don't give these young people a place in our hearts, we won't be worthy of them. We won't be able to change. And they will remain separate from us, isolated in their pain, as if it were all in vain.

The son of Kalonymus Kalman Shapira, the Rebbe of Piaseczno, was murdered in the Holocaust.

In a eulogy for his son, the Rebbe said that God accepted offerings in the Temple in Jerusalem only on condition that the worshipper would confess and seek to change his ways; without a confession, an offering is given in vain.

"So that my son's death will not be in vain," he said, "I declare: My wish is to change."

On this bloodied ground, a model society will rise. We owe it to the fallen and to their families that their sacrifices will not be in vain. For this, we need to open our hearts and let these letters soften them, to pour out tears like water and consent to live and take action in the world with open hearts and with a wish – for change, for brotherhood, and for peace.

Yonatan Dean Haim

Staff Sergeant Yonatan Dean Haim, from Ramat Gan, lone soldier in the Combat Engineering Corps, 603rd Battalion, 7th (Armored) Brigade. He fell in combat in the southern Gaza Strip on the first day of Hanukka, 25 Kislev 5784/ December 8, 2023. He is survived by his parents, four siblings, and a partner. He was twenty-five when he fell.

Yonatan was born as Jonathan in New York to a Christian family. He converted to Judaism, immigrated to Israel, and enlisted in the IDF as a lone soldier.

Two years before his death, Yonatan took a university course on emergency and disaster management, and was exposed to the concept of last letters. This inspired him to leave an envelope with farewell letters to his loved ones, to be in place for any future scenario; he labeled the envelope: "In the event that I die."

Yonatan told his partner, Najma, about the letter. He met her during a Birthright trip to Israel four years before the war. In the letter that he left for his loved ones, in English, he devoted a special paragraph to her in Hebrew.

During the war, Yonatan kept a journal. On November 20, 2023, before he went into Gaza, he wrote a new set of last letters to his family and friends, including a farewell letter to Najma. Three weeks later, Yonatan fell in combat.

One of his friends from the battalion found the journal and passed it on to Najma. The two letters to her are brought here.

Look For Me in the First Rain and the Late Rain

Yonatan Dean Haim

6.6.2022

There's no one else like you, Najma. You can find me everywhere.

Look for me in the early first and the late rain. ***When you see lemons and oranges,*** *you can remember my dreams.*

I loved you more than the world. Our story isn't over; the story is just beginning.

One day you're going to join me in the stars and we'll dance together until dawn.

You'll feel me ***in the Shabbat air by the candles*** *and in the breeze in the middle of the night.*

You can watch me in the swirling storm clouds and know that I'm bringing you water for your beautiful world.

I'm always with you. I love you.

First rain and late rain: A reference to Deuteronomy 11:14.

When you see lemons and oranges: In his conversations with Najma over the years, Yonatan would tell her about his dream to go out to an orange grove and pick oranges straight from the tree. Whenever they passed by the produce market, Yonatan would buy a kilo of oranges and squeeze out fresh juice for the two of them.

After Yonatan's death, Najma decided to plant a huge orange tree in their favorite spot in the Har HaBanim Gardens near their home in Ramat Gan. Next to the tree, she hung a sign:

"The orange tree is in memory of Yonatan Dean Haim,
a lone soldier and city resident who fell in the Swords of Iron War."

In the Shabbat air by the candles: Yonatan was born to a Christian family as Jonathan Dean. During his college studies in New York he made some Jewish friends, was exposed

11.20.2023

Najma,
I love you. Who knew we would become such close friends? I can't believe that we met and connected in ***Nesher****, of all places, ha, but yes, I met the most important person in the whole world… in Nesher. You.*

I was a little afraid to move in with you, but I was also at peace with it because I trust you.

I knew who you were, and the fear of ***moving countries*** *and starting my life in this place disappeared.*

I had strength because I was with you.

Never in my life had I laughed, danced, or smiled that way until I met you.

You give life joy. You're the light in the darkness.

to stories of the Holocaust, and began to get interested in the Hebrew language and in Judaism. In 2020 he completed his conversion process to Judaism, changed his name to Yonatan Haim (Haim means life), and immigrated to Israel on his own.

Yonatan volunteered in Magen David Adom first aid crews and later volunteered to enlist in the IDF, serving in the Combat Engineering Corps.

After he fell in combat, three different funeral services were held for him: a military funeral in Israel, a Jewish funeral in a cemetery in New York, and a Christian funeral in the local church where he was born.

Nesher: Located southeast of Haifa.

Moving countries: On the morning of October 7th, when Yonatan was called up, his family in the US was not yet aware of what was going on in Israel. When Yonatan saw the horrors in the Gaza Envelope, he immediately called his brother Randy and asked him to make sure that their mother wasn't watching the news.

After his death, his brother RJ eulogized him: "He defended his country and his people. He will be remembered in history as someone who died for what he believed in. Jonathan always said, 'I will not rest until this is over; this is my mission, this is my way, and this is what I was called to do.'"

I don't know how I ever got to you here in Israel, but I believe with all my heart that the Creator of the World paved my way to you.

What we have is special.

I give thanks every day that you're in my life; I love to see you in new clothes that you created, with a new hair color, or your smile.

Every time is like the first time, and I stop, and my heart soars over you.

You're so beautiful, intelligent, and special. I hope you have a life full of much happiness and love.

You deserve everything that's good and beautiful in the world.

I'm with you, even from my new home.

I'm waiting for you.

I'm always with you.

אני תמיד איתך.

Yaron Chitiz

Captain Yaron Eliezer Chitiz, from Ra'anana, deputy company commander of the Shaked Battalion, Givati Brigade. He fell in combat in the northern Gaza Strip on 15 Tevet 5784/December 26, 2023. He is survived by his parents, four siblings, and a partner. He was twenty-three when he fell.

Yaron wrote his last letter from Gaza on November 5, 2023, after a week of intense fighting. When he finished writing, he messaged his good friend Eitan: "This won't be relevant, but if it does happen, God forbid, I left a message on my WhatsApp group with myself. You're the only one who knows."

In the eulogy that he gave at Yaron's funeral, Eitan mentioned the letter. After the week of shiva, Yaron's family received his phone and read the letter for the first time.

What a Special, Surreal Country

Yaron Chitiz

Dear, beloved family of mine, Who's supposed to teach twenty-three-year-old kids how to write a letter like this?

What a special, surreal country.... I feel privileged to take part in the country's defense, even if I'm always complaining that my buns ache from sitting in the ***Namer*** *for forty hours straight.*

I feel that I'm a part of the history of the State of Israel that's now being written.

Mom, Dad, Doron, Dandan, Dovie, Yaeli.

Thank you.

Thank you for raising me on sanctifying God's name, loving-kindness, and love of the land.

It's all thanks to you, and to your credit!

If you weren't ***the crazy family that you are,*** *who educated me and never gave up on me and raised me with values and love of the land, I wouldn't be where I am now! (Protecting the country, not in a grave, ha ha.)*

Namer: Literally means tiger. It is an APC (Armored Personnel Carrier).

The crazy family that you are: A year before the war, Yaron and his brothers had already booked a flight, hotel, and tickets for the Euro soccer tournament in Germany.

At Yaron's funeral, his brother Daniel said at his grave: "We planned on flying to the Euro. You have tickets. And I'm wondering how we'll do it." Six months later, Yaron's brothers flew to the game, waving a giant banner with Yaron's picture on it and the words LEGENDS NEVER WALK ALONE.

They posted on social media: "Despite all the sadness – and the sadness never lets up for a moment – promises we keep."

I feel proud to go in and fight Hamas under the banner of the Chitiz family and of Am Yisrael!!!

Thank you for everything; you're a family the State of Israel can be proud of.

*"**Singing and Eulogizing in His Memory**" – Everyone who knows me knows that you're one of the most important things in my life. You're the air that I breathe, the laughter, this true friendship.*

Darah – I love you; you're my life. You give me the strength to go on.

I have no doubt that my future needs to be with you, I really hope that this letter is irrelevant and that we'll get to have many more years together and raise a gorgeous family.

I love you all so much,

Am Yisrael Chai
N.B. Don't embarrass me and send this to Hanoch Daum.

נ.ב. לא לעשות לי בושות ולשלוח לחנוך דאום

"Singing and Eulogizing in His Memory": When one of Yaron's group of friends set out on an adventurous trip to the Far East, his friends joked that there was no way he'd make it back alive, and they changed the name of their WhatsApp group to "Singing and Eulogizing in His Memory."

They talked about everything on the group, which was also fertile ground for dark humor. During the war, Yaron wrote on the group: "I hope that you at least placed some bets. Did anyone bet that I'd die?"

Am Yisrael Chai: "The people of Israel lives," a catchphrase made popular during the late-twentieth-century efforts to free the Jews of the former Soviet Union that is continued to be used today.

N.B. Don't embarrass me and send this to Hanoch Daum: Popular Israeli media personality Hanoch Daum regularly posts about fallen soldiers. This letter was posted on Daum's Facebook page. Dovie, Yaron's brother, sent the letter to Daum, adding: "I debated whether to send my brother's last letter to you because of what he wrote at the end, but if I know him well, he meant exactly the opposite. And if I'm wrong, he's not here to correct me. . . if anyone asks who sent this to you, blame it on my sister."

Eitan Koplovich

Captain (Reserves) Eitan Koplovich, from Hoshaya, officer in the 129th Battalion, 8th (Armored) Brigade. He fell in combat in the Northern Gaza Strip on 9 Sivan 5784/June 15, 2024. He is survived by his wife, son, parents, and five siblings. He was twenty-eight when he fell.

Eitan wrote his last letter in a Word document on his computer on May 31, 2024. He had already completed a first round of reserve duty on the Lebanon border and wrote the letter before a second round of reserve duty in Gaza. He didn't tell anyone about the letter.

Three weeks after he fell in combat, his wife, Yael, happened to find the letter. She opened Eitan's laptop and found an open, unsaved document that began with the words: "If somehow I don't come back."

A Message from Another World – Let It Be Authentic

Eitan Koplovich

If somehow I don't come back

I know, this is the opening for all the pathos and drama
that a dead man can suffuse into the world of the living,
I don't intend to take advantage of it.

First of all, I'm dead, so it isn't supposed to interest me.

Secondly, if this is going to be a message from another
world, let it be authentic.

I didn't love you all *and I don't think that after my*
death you'll all suddenly start loving one another.

I have no interest in volunteer projects, a scenic lookout,
or a promenade in my name.

I feel like our public is tired of memorials.

I didn't love you all: "Eitan knew the typical format of 'fallen soldiers' letters' and chose to write differently," his wife, Yael, says. "It also wouldn't have suited him to be part of this book. The letter that he left, in a file that he didn't even bother saving, feels like thoughts he formulated for himself, and not for the general public. But I still chose to read it at the memorial service a month after Eitan's death, and even to publish it here, because it was important for me to give expression to this different type of voice. I didn't have a paradigm for bereavement. Something in Eitan's singular and different message expressed a lot of emotions for me and gave me a certain comfort. And maybe there's someone else who needs to hear that voice."

Let's embrace the religious rituals – we'll go up and we'll recite a few verses, and we'll go home; like ***Grandpa Koplo****, the moment that you feel like it's a heavy burden and you have to call the nephews to complete the minyan [prayer quorum of ten men] then it's probably the time to stop, and I'll certainly forgive you.*

My Yaeli, you'll always be my best friend. Magic that just won't fade, innocence alongside toughness, strength alongside emotion, ***love alongside more love****. Your character has no contradictions. Everything is perfect to me.*

I remember when we were kids in second or third grade you saw me jumping on the colorful rocks in ***Shelav Gimel****, pretending that the unpainted rocks were lava that I must not fall into; you told me that you do that too sometimes.*

Ruti *died a few weeks after that, and the week after I remember that I came first to class, and you came second, and when you came in I didn't know what to say, because I hadn't encountered death yet, and I said mazal tov [literally, good luck, a blessing of congratulations] that you came back, and you of course got a kick out of*

Grandpa Koplo: Yaakov Koplovich, Eitan's grandfather, had a stroke ten years before the war and afterward was able to communicate with those around him only to a limited degree. He died shortly before Eitan was killed. Eitan loved his grandfather's ethical will, which he saw as humble, as befitted his character.

Love alongside more love: Eitan and Yael met when they were six years old and were soulmates from then until he died. At some point when they were teenagers, romantic love added a level to their deep friendship, and they married at twenty-four.

Shelav Gimel: The third stage of the town's neighborhoods.

Ruti: Ruti, Yael's mother, died of cancer when Yael was seven. At the time, to Eitan she was simply Ruti from the neighborhood, his classmate Yael's mother.

that and said, "Eitan, you don't say mazal tov for things like that," and then I said, "Okay, sorry, so what do you say," and you didn't know either it seems to me.

In any case, even now I don't really have words, we haven't improved much in these aspects of dealing with death. Maybe I'll tell you that you're stronger than you think, or that in certain situations I even feel that I held you back; I believe all that but maybe what's really needed is to make room a bit for this quiet, for a brief moment of silence.

Because maybe the attempt to fill the void with noise, action, speeches, and consolations won't always do good, maybe not – my beauty, it's up to you.

Once, many years ago, I had the thought that if I'd wind up in Grandpa Koplo's condition I wouldn't want to go on.

Approaching the new year I considered that thought selfish. Let me expire painfully and fast at a very old age, after I've completed everything, after all the bonds in my life have faded a bit, when I'll anyhow be a memory to people and not very present in their lives. Let me go after Yael does; let me see Boaz grow up to be a grown-up who can look after me,

and let him give me enough so that he can feel that he's done enough. **Let**

ותן לו לתת לי מספיק כדי שהוא ירגיש שהוא עשה די. תן

Let: "When I read the letter the first time, I was sure it was cut off," his wife explains. "I pressed the Undo buttons in Word again and again, but I couldn't find anything that had been deleted. And I realized that that was it. I think it's a prayer."

Omri Shwartz

Lieutenant Omri Shwartz, from Shadmot Devorah, cadet in the Geffen Battalion, served in the Paratrooper Commando Unit. He fell in combat in the northern Gaza Strip on 8 Tevet 5784/December 20, 2023. He is survived by his parents, brother and sister, and a partner. He was twenty-one when he fell.

Omri wrote a last letter twice.

On October 7th, in the heat of fierce battle to defend Kibbutz Kisufim, Omri and his fellow soldiers took temporary cover from incoming missiles behind an adjacent graveyard. Omri took a small spiral notepad out of his pocket and wrote a farewell letter on its first page.

That notepad became Omri's war journal in Gaza, and he kept writing in it until the day he was killed.

On December 2, 2023, before setting out on a complex mission, Omri wrote a second last letter. Two and a half weeks later, he fell in combat.

On October 14, between writing the two letters, Omri wrote in his journal: "I haven't written for a long time.... I think it's because I sense that the risk of dying has less of a hold on me. I started writing because I wanted to leave behind a freshly written memory of me, but letters aren't for me; that brings the end closer."

I Had a Wild Good Life

Omri Shwartz

10.7.23

We just left Kisufim. We're lying here in the open area behind the graveyard, ***Purple Rain alerts*** *every minute. I'm writing this down here because I realize that* ***the deadly battle we just got through isn't the last****. So I'll write to my family who raised and educated me properly. Mom and Dad I love you; you're the best there is. One couple with one heart, a precisely calibrated combination of heart and mind.*

Noam my brother, you're the salt of this earth and I love you.
Lula my sister, keep everyone sane, since you're the smartest one here.

Purple Rain: A term used in IDF communications for rocket fire and mortar shells.

The deadly battle we just got through isn't the last: That day, Omri fought to defend parts of the Gaza Envelope that were a second home to him. After high school he spent a year volunteering in Kibbutz Be'eri and became very close to the kibbutz members. During the war, whenever he got a few hours of leave, instead of going straight home he went to a hotel at the Dead Sea where the evacuees from Be'eri were staying. On that day, he announced that after he finishes his army service he would move to the kibbutz and make it his home. Omri referred to the war in Gaza as "The Be'eri War."

12.2.23

We're going on a complex raid tonight, but I can't stop smiling. This is what I've been waiting for, this is what I've been training for, I'm part of this country's legacy. Suddenly, it's all clear. ***Our generation, our turn.***

I can't stop smiling because all the experiences I've amassed, and the people with me along the way just won't let me. I couldn't have asked for a better life, nor for more loving parents, nor for a more tight-knit family, nor for a greater beloved, nor for better friends.

Keep laughing and having fun,, *because I had a wild life.*

תמשיכו לצחוק ולהינות,,
אני עשיתי חיים משוגעים.

Our generation, our turn: On December 20, 2023, Omri wrote in his journal: "The war isn't hard – there's food, mattresses, basically everything that's needed. If Grandpa Yaakov managed to make a run for it in frosty Europe with an eight-year-old child on his back, who am I to complain." Mere hours later, he was wounded in battle and bravely continued fighting until he was killed.

Keep laughing and having fun: Inspired by Omri's letter, the artist Yaheli Sobol released the song "Listen Omri," with the words: Listen Omri, / You ordered us to be happy, / But a shiva is a lousy party, / Listen Omri, / On a scale of one to one hundred, / That's a pretty tall order.

Iftah Yavetz

Captain Iftah Yavetz, from Ramat HaSharon, a commander and operations officer in the elite Maglan Commando Unit. He fell in combat on 22 Tishrei 5784/ October 7th 2023. He is survived by his parents and five siblings. He was twenty-three when he fell.

Iftah wrote his letter three months before the war, on July 2, 2023. As an operations officer of the Maglan Commando Unit, he was about to lead the Bayit VeGan [literally "House and Garden"] counter-terror mission into Jenin. The day before the mission, Iftah spoke with one of best friends Goni and confided his feelings facing this complex mission. "My brother, we're doing something historic," he wrote to him. "And I'm the first boots on the ground there."

The next day, a moment before they set out on the mission, Iftah sent his letter to Goni and wrote: "Don't show this to anyone. If something goes wrong today, send this to my parents."

Goni honored his request and told no one about the letter. When Iftah came back safely from Jenin, the two of them went back to their regular routine and made no further mention of the letter.

Three months later, on October 7th, Iftah fell in the battle over Nahal Oz. When he was first notified of his best friend's death, Goni didn't remember the letter placed in his keeping. He only remembered it the next day. He sent the letter to Iftah's parents, who attest that reading it changed their lives.

Suddenly, the Answer Is Very Clear

Iftah Yavetz

Many thoughts are running through my head about ***why us, why now****, why there.*

Tension's in the air, and also dark humor about who will be coming back and who won't.

So many points to keep in mind… to work slowly, to be alert, to keep scanning all the time.

We know what we're about to face; the enemy knows the area and has a lot of surprises in store for us.

In a little while, we'll convene in the staging area for a final briefing before setting out with the clear knowledge (at least to me) that we're embarking on an operation from which not all of us will return.

Despite this, I look behind me and to the sides and I'm very confident in us. We're sharp, we've prepared well, and we've already been in this space several times.

Why us, why now: Mere days before he fell, Iftah sent a letter to his younger sister Tamar, who was about to go on a heritage trip to Poland, and wrote: "I'm writing this letter to you as I'm about to be released after five years in the army, and very soon your turn will come, too, to take part in this unending relay race. It'll keep going with Yael and Dan (and Ella and Michal), and my children, and your children. After this trip you'll probably understand that we have no other country. And this is how we are, generation after generation, swearing that it will never happen again."

I'm trying to imagine the coming hours. To lead this thing, to be the first there in the most complicated part – that's exactly what you educated me to do.

And when my thoughts start to run off a little, why us and why now – that's what I'm thinking about – and suddenly the answer's very clear to me. To fight for this land, to lead this unit – this isn't supreme courage; it's the standard. ***And if I had to sculpt my life all over again, I wouldn't change a thing.***

Love you, Iftah

אוהב אותכם, יפתח

And if I had to sculpt my life all over again, I wouldn't change a thing: "The novel expression Iftah chose, 'to sculpt my life,' perfectly reflects the outlook on life that characterized him," says his mother, Shira. "Life isn't something that happens to him but something that he sculpts with his own hands. Life is a creation, and he is the creator."

Iftah liked to write, and out of the thousands of words that he left behind, it is specifically this phrase that his parents chose to engrave on his tombstone.

"Iftah speaks of himself being at peace with the course of his life and with the choices that he made," his mother explains. "This is the only sentence that can bring me even the smallest measure of consolation when I go to visit him there."

Sufian Dagash

Staff Sergeant Sufian Dagash, from Maghar, served in the Combat Engineering Corps, 601st Battalion, 401st (Armored) Brigade. He fell in combat in the northern Gaza Strip on 21 Tevet 5784/ January 2, 2024. He is survived by his parents and two sisters. He was twenty-one when he fell.

Sufian kept a war journal in a notebook, from the first time he went into Gaza and for the duration of the war.
He wrote his final entry on December 16, 2023; two weeks later, he fell in combat.

Even though Sufian is Druze and his mother tongue is Arabic, he wrote his journal in Hebrew. Sufian's friend kept the journal safe and gave it to his family after he was killed.

I Feel My Whole Body Missing You

Sufian Dagash

10.27.23

Officially I'm going to war

I left the staging area to go past the Gaza fence [...]

It's going to be hard psychologically/physically and from a lot of perspectives. I'm dealing with no few difficulties and everything that's going through my mind is Mom-Dad-Julia-Gina. If only I had talked to them more before I left. Regretting that, and it burns. I don't know if I'm able to keep going, but I do want to finish and go back home healthy and sound, and I'm going to do it for them.

10.29.2023

The third day of the war, or more accurately, of our ground entry into Gaza. I began the morning destroying buildings and terror infrastructures and one very big antenna that actually was cool to bring down.

Now it's 9:51 a.m.
I feel my whole body missing you. I want to get out of here and just go, but we need to destroy this terror organization in order to get back to my life and my family and I'll do anything to get back and if needed I'll flatten Gaza all by myself to get back to them. The first goal in my head is to get back home!!! And for that I'll fight and I'll fight to the end; there's no chance that we're not coming back.

11.15.2023

It's very hard, it's the twentieth day since the war began but until now I didn't feel it and only now it's descending on me in a single boom. I'm scared, I'm afraid, I'm human! Will update later on.

***Shabbat* 12.16.2023**

Day 70 of the war

After months of not seeing home I don't know what I feel anymore…

Tomorrow (Sunday) I'm going home and I'm so happy. I missed Mom, Dad, Julia, Gina, Grandpa, Grandma, uncles, aunts, everybody everybody everybody with no exceptions.

I've seen everything in this war and I also grew up and learned a lot, and all of this has a very heavy price. ***To lose friends*** *and to lose partners in life, and very difficult sights.*

But somehow I kept on going and was sharply focused despite the anger and the longing and the difficulty.

And that's it; ***it's all fun.***

וזהו הכל כיף

To lose friends: Sufian called his father, Khaled, from the heart of Gaza and asked him to go to his friend First Sergeant Gal Hershko's funeral; he wasn't able to get leave from the fighting.

After the funeral, Sufian called his father to make sure that enough people had come. When his father assured him that many had come, Sufian said: "He deserves it. Gal is such a good person, he deserves a lot of people accompanying him on his final journey." Sufian's own funeral was attended by about ten thousand people from all over the country.

It's all fun: Sufian ends what became his last letter with the words "it's all fun," which almost completely contradicts his previous sentences. His father, Khaled, shares that these final words from Sufian give him the strength to keep going.

Moses Wrote with Tears

Rabbanit Yemima Mizrachi

"Look, Yemima!" dozens of bereaved mothers and young widows have said to me this year as they show me a last letter from their loved one.

"Read it," they ask, and their eyes tell me that, more than they want me to read *it*, they want me to read *him* – to reveal something new to them about their loved one, something in his words that they couldn't perceive themselves.

I understand. For years I've tried to decipher the doodles that my little son, who was very ill, drew on my *Humash* when I was preparing to teach, but he's no longer here to tell me what his pictures meant. Through these mysterious scrawls, my child left me with enormous freedom to piece together the story of his life, the story of his death.

I'm reminded of my son's doodles when I stand before the last words of the casualties of the war. And I try, I try so hard, to read beyond the fleeting letters, to smell the burnt parchment and to bring tidings from that other world to the mother who's here longing for them....

Each time anew, I discover that when fighters leave final words behind, they are constructing a new secret code, a code secret even to them, since they are writing about a reality that they've never experienced. A reality in which they are no more.

What did they want from this last letter of theirs?

They intended for us to turn their words over, again and again. They imagined us imagining them writing. They wanted us to understand that, when they wrote about the moment when they'd no longer be here, they thought about only one thing: about us.

About the mother who would cling to these words like a legacy; about the father who would be so proud; about the loved one left behind; about their people, *Am Yisrael*, for whom they fought. They wanted all of them to know one thing, in the words of poet Natan Yonatan: "He must have loved me, that man."

In the last words that soldiers – male and female – leave behind, they seek not to be heroes in death. They seek to be heroes of life.

By writing about the possibility of their deaths, they are not tempting death, but defying it, sticking out their tongue at it, attempting to confuse it and send it off to another place, as by sleight of hand.

These fighters are the only people in the whole world who yearn for what they wrote with their own blood to never be read.

*

Last words are no less than Torah, demanding contemplation and study. This is exactly how the first last words in our history were written: in the Torah.

At the end of the Torah, at the edge of the wilderness, eight final verses appear, opening with the words "And there died Moses, servant of the Lord."

The Sages turn these words over again and again, trying to understand how Moses, who wrote the entire Torah, Moses, the man of truth whose Torah is truth, could write words about himself that cannot be true: "And there died Moses"? But a dead man cannot write!

"Can it be that Moses was alive and wrote, 'And there died Moses, servant of the Lord?'" the Sages ask in the Talmud, and they answer: "Rather, until here, God dictates and Moses writes; from here on – God dictates and Moses writes with tears" (Bava Batra 15a).

The Sages explain that Moses writes down these last verses as he weeps.

The Ritva, a renowned thirteenth-century exegete, adds his own moving interpretation: "'Writes with tears'; unlike the entire Torah, which was written with ink, Moses wrote these last eight verses with his very tears."

Wow. Moses wrote the rest of the Torah with black ink, but the Ritva relates that Moses wrote the final verses with a clear ink, an invisible ink – his tears.

Moses wept. Moses wept a lot. He wept because of how much he loved life. Throughout the Torah, Moses – who fought bravely against the Emorite, Amalek, King Sihon – writes about the value of life. His whole life he dreamt of redemption, of freedom, of a life of liberty in the Promised Land. And precisely because of this, he writes his final message, preparing to die outside of the Land, with tears.

The Sages reveal to us that Moses, with his last words, asks that we not forget him. That we remember his tremendous sacrifice, the fact that he did all he could to see us to victory, to see life flourishing in the Land, though he did not merit to see it.

"He said to them, 'Please, when you come into the Land, remember me,'" (Midrash Deuteronomy Rabba, *Va'ethanan*).

This is a basic human message, not manipulative but practically pleading: Please, remember me!

When you dwell, every man under his vine and under his fig tree, in days of peace, remember that I played a significant part in bringing about this peace – the peace I so wanted you to achieve, that I longed to experience along with you. Remember that I gave my whole life for the life of this people.

*

Natan Yonatan wrote a marvelous poem about last words – words of love that are read in darkness.

He wrote these words before the Yom Kippur War. Only looking back, after he lost his son Lior in that war, did he discover that he, too, had written in code without realizing it.

If a painful crown of thorns
is the very thing you love
to the desert I will go
there to study pain.
And were you to love poems
only when written in granite –
I'd live among the crags
and on the rocks I'd write.

Then, when we've covered up
with the sands in darkness
and the chronicle
with dark has covered up,
you will tell me words
more fair than tears or gladness;
it seems he must have
loved me, this very man.

And I want to add another line to this poem, with tears:
"He must have loved living, that man."

Shachar Fridman

Staff Sergeant Shachar Fridman, from Jerusalem, served in the 101st Battalion, Paratroopers' Brigade. He fell in the northern Gaza Strip on 5 Kislev 5784/November 18, 2023. He is survived by his parents, three sisters, and a spouse. He was twenty-one when he fell.

Shachar wrote two last letters.

The first, to his parents, was written on October 27th before he went into Gaza. He sent the letter to his friend Itai, and sent his mother's phone number in the next message.

He wrote the second in the Notes app on his phone on October 29, 2023, two days before he went into Gaza. He sent it to his spouse, Noga, and wrote: "Don't stress out from this. It's just something I wrote now after a few things I had here. It's not a eulogy or anything; it's just a kind of agenda."

Shachar wrote the letter after participating in intense combat in the Gaza Envelope on October 7th. In a video interview with him at the beginning of the war, he said: "The horrors I saw helped me find my 'why.'" About two weeks after he wrote the letter, Shachar fell in combat. That day, his friend Itai forwarded the first letter to his parents.

The second letter that Shachar sent to Noga, "just a kind of agenda," has been translated into many languages and shared all over the world.

Aside from these two letters, Shachar found a red notebook in Gaza and decided to start writing. Between battles, he kept a journal interspersed with love letters to Noga. "A person who had never really written before suddenly left behind a twenty-six-page treasure," says Noga. Israeli singer Marina Maximillian Blumin wrote the song "Noga," based on Shachar's journal.

I Fought for You to Live, Not Survive

Shachar Fridman

10.27.23

To my dear parents,

Who always supported me and loved me no matter what, who fought like lions for me and never cut me slack on the way to the goal –

of becoming the best person I could be – I hope that I managed to fulfill it as much as possible.

I love you more than anything and appreciate you no end for everything you did for me. In my mind I treasure every single moment we had together, both good and bad, for all of them brought us here.

You're my best friends *and it's crazy fun for me to be with you! I was greatly privileged to have our dynamic and our friendship now and I'm so grateful for that.*

I hope – I'm sure – that later on, we'll read this letter together in the yard over some good beer and a cigarette and laugh and make plans for the future and you'll raise

You're my best friends: In the war journal he kept in Gaza, Shachar wrote in a paragraph dedicated to his father:

"Dad, it's Friday again, and again it brings up a yearning for our beautiful Shabbat moments, and I'm choking back the tears that want to come out. How much fun it would be if, say, I had gotten out of Gaza yesterday morning and now we were sitting at evening prayers and I wouldn't stop talking and you'd be listening and every so often saying shhhh! So that we'd actually pray for a second and then we'd go back to talking.

I miss you, Dad. I hope that we'll be able to sit together soon and laugh about it all, even *an eyebrow at my plans. But if not, then I beg of you, in every way – I fought so that my family and friends and I could live! For you to live! Not for you to survive, not for you to breathe and exist, for you to live fully – so do it!*

Travel all over the world in my name and do crazy things, go out to dance as much as possible like I loved to, listen to a variety of special music, and love life; appreciate the little things that make our lives special – when a good song pops up on shuffle or the radio, when the weather is perfect for the beach or for a natural spring in the middle of the day and you jump into the water, even if it's for ten minutes.

Simply live life to the fullest.

You should know that even if, God forbid, I fell in battle and everything seems black, I'm sitting on high and smiling because I chose this. Thanks to the education that I received, I came to the realization that if I truly want to live I need to suffer a bit now – a brief descent for the sake of an ascent.

***I was called to protect the flag** and no one is happier about this than I am! I'm happy to have had the privilege*

though most of what's here isn't funny... there's crazy divine protection here, you should know, or maybe they're just really incompetent, a lot of anti-tank missiles have already whistled by my ear. What can I tell you; God has plans for me yet."

I was called to protect the flag: On October 7th, Shachar waged fierce battle in the Gaza Envelope. "There's no one here who doesn't have a friend who was killed," Shachar said in an interview after the fighting. "When soldiers usually go on leave, their fantasy is to eat shawarma. Our fantasy is to get to the graves of the friends we've lost.

I love this country and I truly love my people, each and every one. I don't care about religion, race, color, or gender.

They badmouthed this generation, 'the TikTok generation', but there are acts of courage here. I have a friend [Aner Shapira, 22, threw back seven live grenades tossed into a bomb shelter near Kibbutz Re'im by Hamas terrorists. He saved multiple lives before being killed *of securing peace and quiet for my family and my friends and for every member of Am Yisrael. If I have to sacrifice my life so that you and* **my sisters** *and grandparents can sleep well at night, without sirens, and won't need to fear terror attacks and can live in peace – I fully accept and am at peace with that.*

In any case, I'm a pro in a company of "machines" [a nickname for highly skilled soldiers], and I'm absolutely sure that nothing will hit me, but in case I fail to keep my promise, I didn't want not to leave some words behind me, I mean, you know how much I love to talk...

In conclusion – thank you truly truly. I love and appreciate you more than anything!

Live!!

by the eighth grenade]; he stood at the entrance of a mobile shelter, grabbed grenades as they threw them, and threw them back out. It's a different generation. We've proven ourselves. On the first day of the war, my commander said, 'I'm prepared to die.' I'm like him. I'm prepared to die for the sake of our country."

Two weeks later, Shachar and his commander, Jamal Abbas, fell together in combat in Gaza.

My sisters: Shachar also wrote in his diary to his big sister Noya. "Ah my twin, 'we don't want to sleep, we want to go wild' [from the chorus of "The Neighborhood Song," an Israeli comedy song from the 1960s.]? My Non, I want to sleep; who would have believed that your baby brother would write you from the heart of Gaza. Oh God, you'd go nuts here; the smell is awful. I miss you my sister; you and I are connected by an invisible string, no? Remember when Dad would read *Hassamba* (a classical Israeli children's adventure series) to us? We always wanted to be heroes like them – it's sort of like that, no?"

10.29.23

Be good people. *Smile. Aspire to make everyone you meet smile, too. Be open to criticism and always try to improve.*

Know that the greatest quality a person can have is the capacity to make another person happy. Open your ears to the needs of your fellow man, and open your eyes to his pain.

Try and smile as much as you can, even when it's tough. Pay attention to the little people who come into the periphery of our vision.

Appreciate the little things that the world has to offer, *especially nature and music.*

Be good people: Here Shachar used an elevated, archaic form of the word "be." "The first time I read these words, I searched the internet for the original text he was quoting," his mother, Liat, shares. "It's written in a very high register. What kind of twenty-one-year-old kid writes 'be' in that form?"

"Today I realize that he grew up all at once. The horrors he witnessed suddenly brought out all his inner DNA. Instead of writing about despair, disappointment, or fear, he chose to write 'Be good people.' That was what Shachar always demanded from the world – and from himself."

Appreciate the little things that the world has to offer: Shachar found an old transistor radio in Gaza during the fighting and fixed it. In the lulls between battles, he would listen to music on it. He wrote in his journal: "I'm sitting on a chair in the living room with a small flashlight and talking to my mother. 'Drive Slowly' [a classic Israeli seventies soft rock song by Arik Einstein, tracing a man's thoughts as he keeps himself steady at the

And most important—be good people in your own way. Don't let society dictate to you what makes you good people – just try as hard as possible; and even when you fall, know that this is the route to success.

Love yourselves and the world, and when you radiate joy outward –
slowly, slowly, it will create a circle that will create a better world.

ייווצר לאט לאט מעגל שייצר עולם טוב יותר.

wheel as it rains] is playing in the background on batteries and the army radio is to my left, but when I'm talking to Mom it's all background noise. Today, at 20:00, I felt that you were hugging me and sending me strength. And just then, the song changed: 'My chicks have flown the nest' [the first line of another song by Einstein, from the late eighties, sung from the perspective of a mother bird wishing her chicks well as they venture forth into life]."

In a paragraph in his diary devoted to his partner, Noga, Shachar wrote: "In one of the temporary, locations today, when we were waiting to go in to attack, I picked basil and lemons, I smoked tuna and added salted peanuts. It reminded me: When I get back, I'll make fish for you the way you like. Love you."

Yair Roitman

Sergeant Yair Roitman, from Karnei Shomron, combat soldier-in-training in the Givati Commando Unit. He was critically injured in combat in the southern Gaza Strip on June 10, 2024, and died from his wounds on 9 Sivan 5784/ June 15, 2024. He is survived by his parents and five siblings. He was nineteen when he fell.

Yair wrote his last letter by hand on May 28, 2024 before going back into Gaza, and left the page with his company sergeant-major. To be on the safe side, he also photographed the letter and saved the image in a hidden album on his phone.

Yair was critically injured in combat. After five days of fighting for his life, he succumbed to his wounds.

On the first day of his shiva, Yair's company sergeant-major visited his parents and gave them the letter.

I Decided to Write for the Sake of One More Memory

Yair Roitman

With God's Help

5.28.24

My dear family, I hope you never need to open this letter.

I didn't even want to write this because it'd be bad luck, but I decided to write for the sake of one more memory and maybe even a smile, and so that you'll know how much I love you and want to say thank you for every minute of my life, for every smile you gave me.

And I want to ask you **not to be sad because of me***. That I should only be a memory that gives you strength no matter what you do, and I'll be happy to see your successes here from up above.*

And I want **to ask forgiveness if I hurt you at some point***, and only want you to keep doing good.*

Here with you always, Yair

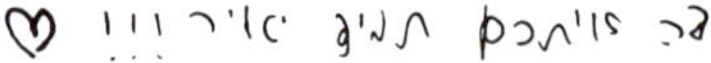

Not to be sad because of me: After Yair lost a close friend, he called his three best friends and made them swear that if something would happen to him, they would support his parents and make sure that they wouldn't sink into sadness.

To ask forgiveness if I hurt you at some point: Yair grew up in a religious home to parents who were both educators, and throughout his life he chose a different path from theirs. Yair had a complicated relationship with religion, and at the beginning of high school he dropped out and started a successful food-truck.

Despite their differences, Yair maintained a strong, loving relationship with his parents and did his best not to hurt them. Only in the hospital, after he was wounded, did his father discover that he had a phrase tattooed on his chest: "If you don't try, you won't succeed." Tattoos are prohibited in Jewish law, based on Leviticus 19:28.

"He hid the tattoo from us for all those years so as not to hurt us," his father says. "That made me happy. He did what he wanted, and still he was a righteous one, a *tzaddik*. Even in his last letter, the first word that he wrote was the acronym for, 'with God's help.' It seems that that's where his heart was, completely."

Lavi Lipshitz

Staff Sergeant Lavi Lipshitz, from Modiin Maccabim-Reut, served in the Givati Commando Unit. He was killed in combat in the northern Gaza Strip on 16 Heshvan 5784/ October 31, 2023. He fell at the age of twenty and is survived by his parents and three siblings.

Lavi wrote his letter six months before the war broke out. In April 2023 he was about to begin a period of operational deployment, and was concerned that something significant was about to occur. Lavi saved his letter in a folder entitled "IDF" on his computer, under the name "In Case I Die."

On October 10, 2023, when he left Nahal Oz after three days of intense fighting, he sent a message to his sister Anafa, explaining that if anything should happen to him, a letter awaited the family on his computer.

Three weeks later, Lavi fell in combat in Jabalia. He was the first soldier killed during the ground maneuvers in Gaza. That evening, the family read the letter for the first time.

I'd Better Leave Operating Instructions

Lavi Lipshitz

This may be the beginning of a third Lebanon War. *I thought it would be worthwhile to leave behind a few explanations.*

In case I die, ***I'd better leave operating instructions*** *or some sort of eulogy about myself. After all, what's the point of living if I don't get to eulogize anyone?*

I do not regret enlisting in the Givati Bridgade's Commando Unit *or Squad 3, my unit. In fact, I am grateful for that. The opportunity to make friends like the people I encountered in the military is remarkable. Thank you to the country for giving me*

This may be the beginning of a third Lebanon War: Lavi served as an operations officer in the Orev division of the Givati Commando Unit and was an inquisitive soldier with expert knowledge of operational plans, and awareness of dangers. "In that time period, on the basis of his personal understanding, Lavi was afraid of a significant event," his father, Nitzan, explains. "He writes 'a third Lebanon War' as an extreme metaphor for something big, in which he was liable to lose his life."

I'd better leave operating instructions: In his letter, Lavi included detailed instructions for his family. The family chose to leave this section of the letter private.

I do not regret enlisting in the Givati Brigade's Commando Unit: Lavi was an artist, a cinephile, and a gifted photographer. After two weeks in the army, Lavi said to his father, Nitzan, "Dad, I'm leaving. They want to turn me into a war machine, and I'm not like that."

His father said to him, "Lavi, one day you'll go out to save people. What you will do is save people."

On October 7th Lavi was deployed in the Gaza Envelope and fought in the battles for Kibbutz Nahal Oz. The next day, he wrote to his father: "Wow, you had to see the faces of people when we came to rescue them, it's unbelievable."

When he came out of Nahal Oz, after rescuing dozens of people, he said to his mother, Shlomit: "Mom, someone is taking care of the Israelis, but who'll take care of the foreign workers who don't know what came upon them? My heart breaks to see the cows in the cowshed. Who will come to milk them?"

this opportunity and ***thank you to my friends for giving me the chance for such an extraordinary bond.***

[…]

Finally, I ask you not to drown in grief. Grief may be daily and exhausting, yet the activity that may grow out of it is not exhausting, but constructive.

Thank you to my friends for giving me the chance for such an extraordinary bond: During his army service, Lavi produced a booklet of photos called "Team" in which he documented his friends and wrote about what made each of them unique. In his introduction to the booklet, he wrote: "In my first days of basic training I felt like an outsider, like I didn't belong, rejected, a starling in a flock of ravens." Lavi's unit was Orev, literally, the "Ravens" unit.

"I was helped a lot by thinking about Adi Nes's photos (prominent Israeli photographer), about the endless desert surrounding me, and about the question of how and when I'd get back to photography.

Over this time period, I understood how, on the one hand, being different from the group is what preserved my identity, but on the other hand, it was what distanced me from them.

After some time and daily conversation with members of the platoon, it became clear that I'm not the only one who doesn't belong to the group. Rather there are thirty-five individuals who don't belong to the group, but at the same time, they are *the* group.

This observation helped me realize that the overall uniformity the army forces upon us is also what makes our personalities distinct.

This understanding led a decision to form in my heart – I must make a record of the individualism that this uniformity creates.

As a result I began to compose photos that would capture the uniqueness of each of my friends on the team but at the same time would display their part in this unbreakable weave.

After about fourteen months of lead-up and another six months of processing experiences, my artistic creation was born."

Nothing has been more difficult for me than doing nothing, *so I ask everyone around me – always do.*

Lavi Lipshitz

a e

h h

s a

h a

o m

v i

n

לביא ליפשיץ

Nothing has been more difficult for me than doing nothing: "Lavi was a person of action who found time for everything," says his mother, Shlomit. "He gave up sleep and meals to do things that were important to him: photography, reading, helping people." Up until the day before the war, Lavi maintained a successful Instagram account called "till_when_photo_diary" with the description "I'm a poor fighter and suffering artist who posts a daily photo taken by me in the IDF. Givati Orev, enjoy!"

Lavi planned to study art at Israel's Betzalel Academy of Arts and in New York to become a professional photographer and cinematographer. In a phone call with his father about the difficult sights he saw on October 7th, they joked that even Quentin Tarantino, his favorite film director, couldn't have conjured up what Lavi saw with his own eyes.

Lavi: In a letter he wrote to himself at the beginning of tenth grade which was to be opened at the graduation from high school, Lavi signed his name horizontally, but added two words descending vertically from his initials: Lahshov, Lehaamin – to think, to believe.

Matan Vinogradov

Staff Sergeant Matan Vinogradov, from Jerusalem, served in the 932nd Battalion, Nahal Brigade. He fell in combat in the northern Gaza Strip on 8 Adar Bet 5784/March 18, 2024. He is survived by his mother and sister. He was twenty when he fell.

Matan wrote his last letter on October 15, 2023, in the Notes app on his phone, as the IDF were preparing to begin their ground operations in Gaza. A week later, he sent his sister Stella the password to his phone, and wrote, “I hope you won’t need to use this.”

After he fell in combat, Matan’s family opened the locked cell phone and found his last letter, under the title “Will.”

Stronger Than a Tank

Matan Vinogradov

If you're reading this, I must either be mortally wounded or dead.

Stella, Mom, and Grandma, I ask you not to cry; if this happened this was meant to happen.

In the end, I was killed for the sake of safeguarding civilians and I hope that Hamas no longer exists and that Hezbollah understands the might of Israel and its allies; everything is from Heaven and for the ultimate good, because in the end after every fall there is a rise, and our people have experienced many ups and downs.

We survived Egypt, the Babylonian exile, two thousand years of exile with innumerable persecutions of Jews, and in the end even ***the Holocaust, in which our own family suffered,*** *and fought against the Nazis. Today we're fighting against a different and worse type of Nazi, the kind that beheads babies. These terrorists deserve death and they must be wiped off the earth. We must not repeat the mistake we made in 2004, for Judea and Samaria would be 10 or 20 or 10,000 times worse.*

But please, drop that; it matters more to me to tell you things that I hope will make you proud, and a few other things I ask of you.

The Holocaust, in which our own family suffered: Matan was from a family of Ukrainian immigrants, and his grandmother Yelena was one of the most significant people in his life. In his childhood, he would visit her every day after school, cook for her, and spend hours with her. Yelena suffered terrible abuse from the Nazis as a young child, survived, and raised a family in Israel. Matan grew up on her stories, and saw his war as part of that same history.

The personal equipment I fought with is a grenade launcher that shoots sixty grenades a minute. You might say that it's stronger than a tank, and therefore I'm afraid that I'm ***a high-value target for Hamas and its snipers.***

Not only that, but our goal is to conquer all of Gaza, which will take a lot of time and resources.

Okay, now for dividing up my belongings. ***The computer goes to Noam*** *or to the family in general.*

My phone is for Orian.

At the moment I have [...] in savings and in my checking account.

I ask that at least 20 percent (like my age) go to charities that save lives; leave the rest for yourselves and divide it up so that you have money for emergencies.

The VR headset and controllers are also for Noam and Orian.

A high-value target for Hamas and its snipers: Matan volunteered to be the grenadier and carry the heavy, powerful grenade launcher. He describes its efficacy in the hope of making his family proud. Matan wants them to know that if he is killed, it is a sign that he was a significant fighter, in his words: "a high-value target for Hamas."

The computer goes to Noam: Matan had a seven-year-old nephew, Noam, and a four-year-old niece, Orian. "Matan was the best uncle in the world," his sister and brother-in-law share. "When we worked shifts, he was the one who raised them."

Matan was a serious gamer. He and Noam shared a virtual world in Minecraft and played it together for long hours. Matan asked to leave his professional gaming equipment to Noam so that he would be able to keep playing. Today, Noam continues to build out the world they once built together.

The furniture take for yourselves.

Give my Steam account to Gavriel*; he has Mom's phone number. She already sent him a photo of the password and everything.*

Legacy: ***I'd be very happy if they'd set something up in my memory*** *that would help people a lot and that would be long term, something like education; donors aren't lacking.*

N.B. This was written on 10/15/23. Maybe I'll update this here but this is it for now. Additionally, when there are ground maneuvers I'll write down in my journal for them to bring us a summary of my days there in battle and what the situation was ***so that you know what happened with me there****; it'll be in my combat bag, in the top pocket when you open the bag's main compartment; it'll probably be classified but keep it.*

I hope I'm writing this for nothing and you won't need to read this

מקווה שאני אכתוב את זה לשווא ולא תצטרכו
לקרוא את זה

Give my Steam account to Gavriel: Steam is a popular gaming platform. Matan bequeathed his personal account, which is worth a large sum of money, to his best friend, Gavriel, who shared his love of gaming.

I'd be very happy if they'd set something up in my memory: Matan's family undertook to fulfill his request. They looked for a project that would combine what he asked for – "charities that save lives. . . . something like education" – and decided to raise money for an educational center in the Schneider Children's Hospital Intensive Care Unit. Within three days, they met their target of 150,000 shekels. Matan's school network, "Shuvu," dedicated a classroom to his memory, commemorating him and his great loves -- education and children.

So that you know what happened with me there: In Gaza, Matan kept a detailed journal of his war experiences, day after day. His family is currently editing it for publication as a book.

Joseph Gitarts

Sergeant First Class (Reserves) Joseph (Yosef) Gitarts, from Tel Aviv, combat soldier in the 7029th Armored Battalion of the 179th Brigade. He fell in combat in the southern Gaza Strip on 13 Tevet 5784/December 25, 2023. He is survived by his parents and four siblings. He was twenty-five when he fell.

When Joseph was debating whether to write a last letter, he called his older brother Zev. Zev, who fought in Operation Defensive Shield, told him that this was a decision that a person has to make for himself.

Joseph decided to write, and sent the letter on November 11, 2023. To make sure that it would be read only in the event of his death, Joseph, who was a programmer, encoded it. He wrote the letter on a Google Doc and split the link to it into two. He sent half the link to his long-time friend, Maria, and the second half to his brother, Zev. But Maria and Zev both couldn't open the Google Doc, and they both also didn't know who was entrusted with the other half of the link. They only had the one instruction from Joseph – only if something would happen to him – to send the link to his mother.

After Joseph's death, his mother, Larisa, received both halves of the link and was able to open the letter. She put them together and read the letter for the first time.

Joseph, who immigrated to Israel at age thirteen, wrote his letter in Russian. His brother Zev translated it into Hebrew.

I Never Feared Death

Joseph Gitarts

Dear Mom and Dad,

I love you very much. Everything is as it has to be. I chose this myself.

I lived a good and interesting life. At the same time, I never feared death.

If, from the perspective of this moment, there is no difference between an event that occurred a minute ago or a decade ago, then there won't be a difference in another seventy years regarding when I died.

We live in four dimensions; therefore all future events already exist, just like Moscow still exists while we are in Israel.

I've even always wondered a bit at the importance that people ascribe to death.

I could have not gone here and hidden.

But that would have gone against everything I believe in and value, and who I consider myself to be.

Therefore I had no choice, and I would do the same thing even if I could make the choice anew.

I made this decision myself and went with it to the end. I fell with honor for the sake of my people. I have no regrets.

I could have not gone here and hidden: At three different points in his army service, before and during the war, Joseph chose the more difficult path. He repeatedly challenged discharges he received for bureaucratic and medical reasons and insisted on joining battle as a combat soldier.

I love you very much and am proud that you're my parents. You gave me a great deal. ***I had an interesting****, rich, happy, unique* ***life****.*

My death only highlights this.

I'm completely thrilled to have lived for twenty-five special years instead ***of living for eighty regular years*** *like everyone else.*

I'm not like everyone else*. I'm stronger. Thanks to you, I got to be like this.*

You are surely in great pain. But you'll get over that. I would very much like that. This is the main thing that I want.

You both have many people close to you who will support you. Please find something positive in all this. Be with the grandchildren.

Help Israel. I'm okay.

תעזרו לישראל. אני בסדר.

I had an interesting life: During the war, Joseph faced a logistical challenge: How can you fit a thick book into a tank driver's crowded compartment, when everything that goes into it is measured to the centimeter? As an avid reader, Joseph wasn't willing to give up his thick books, so he found a creative solution: He divided a book into separate sections and was able to find a place for each of them to fit in the compartment.

I'm not like everyone else: Joseph was a gifted mathematician who devoted his career to research in the field of healthy life extension. Together with a group of researchers, he worked to ensure that science would give people more years of active and full life, free from disease – and the results of his work were published in leading American journals. He had nearly completed his doctoral dissertation and had prepared a business plan for a start-up.

To Look Fear in the Eye

Avi Issacharoff, journalist and screenwriter

A few years ago, when I was moving house, I suddenly found a bundle of old letters wrapped in yellowed paper, inscribed:

"To T, in the event that."

These were letters I had written to a former girlfriend a few months after our breakup, when I was deep into service as an undercover operative in the Duvdevan Unit, with no shortage of clashes and danger lurking in every direction.

I began to write these letters following an injury I had from an encounter with a band of Hamas terrorists in Hebron, which, in a sense, put the fear of death into me.

My injury was light, but in the moments after getting wounded, when my condition wasn't yet clear and my consciousness began to fade, a whole train of thought passed through my head. About my ex-girlfriend and my parents, about my sisters and friends. And one thought crystallized and troubled me, and perhaps was what kept me awake: How, for God's sake, could I not have written any parting words for them? How could it be that I'd never actually be able to tell them, her, anyone, what I wanted to say but never got around to saying?

Soldiers train month after month for going out to battle; they prepare for combat. But nothing truly prepares them for the moment when fear comes by, seeping into the subconscious, into the unconscious.

For some, it's "just" a rush of adrenaline. For others, it's a very real fear. Fear of death, of the unknown, of leaving all the people that you really loved.

This feeling became far more common on October 7th and has been a continuous presence ever since, not relaxing its grip. In Gaza, Lebanon, Syria, Judea and Samaria, a new generation of fighters has shown itself as lions, as superheroes. Except that these superheroes, the ones from real life, experience fear and know how to keep functioning, taking action and charging forward, although the fear is always there. The new Middle East security order has forced these fighters into situations where they know there's a considerable chance of getting injured or even, God forbid, killed. And they are forced to contend with this surreal reality, the new life of a soldier, model 2023-24.

And yes, I can only imagine that almost all of them have a real need to leave something to the world. To say something you never said. Or something you already said, but that it's important to you to say again. Even for the hundredth – or perhaps even for the thousandth – time, you want your girlfriend or partner or wife (or boyfriend or husband) to know how much you loved them, how you would give everything to spend one more happy moment with them, for another second of unadulterated love. You might want to ask forgiveness of those you hurt, or send a sign of life to those you miss already and cannot see again.

It's not just another will, the kind you make as an adult to leave something for the kids. For some of these writers, it was important to leave some kind of message, primarily one of optimism, of joy. It was important to them that their families, their loved ones, wouldn't give up on life because of their deaths; that they wouldn't give up on light and sink into darkness.

There are also those who sought to express a more general, even political, message. About the possibility of falling captive and about their desire for a better society, one that also knows how to show respect for the weak and to hear the voiceless. Or, as Shachar Fridman wrote in his last letter, which I loved so much: "Pay attention to the little people who come into the periphery of our vision. Appreciate the little things that the world has to offer, especially nature and music." These aren't the words of a young man, a boy of twenty-one, even though that was Shachar's age when he was killed. These are the words of a person with a mature, solid, complete worldview. That was his charge to the public, but he also had other words to write, personal words to Noga, his love, words that he didn't want to be his last, but that became his last when he was killed.

And there are no few letters that ask for forgiveness. Not for specific actions, but for these superheroes' very decisions to become combat soldiers. To knowingly endanger their lives, with the understanding that there was a real possibility that those around them, their parents and families, might have to pay the highest price of all. They ask forgiveness for not coming back, for no longer being by their side, because they decided to protect their homeland and sacrifice their lives for *Am Yisrael*.

But you're not the ones who need to ask forgiveness of us. We "grown-ups" need to ask forgiveness of you, of this generation.

We're sorry that we thought that you were a bit spoiled, less principled than previous generations. We're sorry that we sometimes called you the "TikTok generation," you whose deeds have proven that you're on par with the soldiers of the War of Independence in 1948.

So at least in my name – Avi – and perhaps in the name of many others – I want here to ask forgiveness of you, the fallen, those who wrote last letters and those who did not. I'm sorry that we didn't see who you truly were. That we didn't know what you were made of until the moment you stood the test, leaving us speechless. Forgive us, and may we learn to be worthy of the sacrifice you made.

Oriya Yaakov

Staff Sergeant Oriya Yaakov, from Ashkelon, served in the 614th Battalion, Combat Engineering Corps Training School. He fell in combat in the northern Gaza Strip on 29 Kislev 5784/ December 12, 2023. He is survived by his parents, four siblings, and a partner. He was twenty when he fell.

Oriya wrote his last letter in the Notes app on his phone on the evening he went into Gaza, at the beginning of the IDF's ground operations.

He told a few friends about the letter, as well as his twelfth-grade teacher, with whom he'd kept in close contact. The teacher came to Oriya's memorial service a month after his death and gave his parents their son's last letter.

What Fun, Everyone Came Out for Me

Oriya Yaakov

Mom, Dad, Whazz-up? What fun, everyone came out for me,

Listen, I ask you not to cry over me too much.

I did what I really wanted to!

With strength from you, I went to defend our country and hit the enemy!

I was exactly where I wanted to be my entire army service.

I know that it's sad and hard to say goodbye,

But I went for the sake of my people, and you, my family, are part of my people, just as the nation is inseparable, you are not taking leave of me – we'll always remain part of this eternal people.

It was clear to me that I was going to a dangerous place, but that didn't concern me at all; I had only one thought in my mind! That not another hair would be harmed on another Jew's head!

I did what I really wanted to: When Oriya was in the staging area before entering Gaza, his mother told him on the phone that since October 7th, she had been praying to God every morning, asking Him: Please, don't make him go into Gaza.

"Mom, stop praying for that," he asked her, "I'm praying for the opposite. Every morning, when I put on my tefillin [phylacteries] here, I pray that I'll have the privilege of going in to fight. I want to defend the country."

You saw how ***hundreds of people I don't even know came to my funeral****, they all came to show their appreciation and pay their respects for my death; everyone stood with an Israeli flag and heads held high in the face of our enemies and joined in the funeral procession.*

Grandma and Grandpa who immigrated from Kurdistan and Yemen could only dream of being soldiers in the Jewish army of the Jewish state.

I fulfilled the dream for them!

How much have we suffered! How much have we been injured, and today, blessed be God, we came back to our country!

Jewish blood isn't worthless as it was in the exile, in the pogroms, in the terrible Holocaust. In the Farhud in Iraq masses of Jews were murdered and no one avenged their blood; likewise in Yemen, in Tunisia, and in many other lands.

The State of Israel and the Israeli Defense Forces changed the equation.

I'm proud to be part of that change in the equation.

Mom and Dad, please continue the legacy, give strength to the family, give strength to the special people to which you belong!

Hundreds of people I don't even know came to my funeral: Just as Oriya imagined, many Israelis who didn't know him came to Ashkelon with Israeli flags to accompany him on his final journey. "He asked for hundreds," says his father, "and he got thousands."

I ask you not to sink deeply into sorrow; they say that the greatest sorrow to the deceased is his family's sorrow. I ask you to be strong.

I'm up above next to the Throne of Glory, the closest to the Master of the World, together with all the souls of the soldiers and terror victims; the souls are all sitting and praying to strengthen the people of Israel in its fight for its land, for its unity, for its state.

"The Strength of Israel will not lie or repent" *and* ***just as our father Jacob didn't die, for his seed lives,*** *we, too, will merit to continue our lives as a people in our own country.*

Love you!

אוהב אתכם!

The Strength of Israel will not lie or repent: I Samuel 15:29.

Just as our father Jacob didn't die, for his seed lives: This is a reference to the Babylonian Talmud, Taanit 5b. At the same time that Oriya's funeral was held, another life cycle event was taking place in Ashkelon: a ritual circumcision. The baby's parents didn't know Oriya Yaakov and hadn't heard about his death, but they happened to name their son Oriya Yaakov. After the new parents heard about the death of the soldier Oriya Yaakov, they went to pay respects to the family and told them this story. The families have been in close contact ever since.

Nir Hadad

Sergeant First Class (Reserves) Nir Hadad, from Petach Tikva, combat soldier in the 8th Armored Brigade's 129th Battalion. He was critically injured in combat in the northern Gaza Strip on June 15, 2024 and died of his wounds on 4 Tishrei 5785/October 6, 2024. He is survived by his wife, two daughters, mother, and five siblings. He was twenty-eight when he fell.

Nir wrote his last letter in his WhatsApp group with himself, on June 5, 2024, the day before his first entry into Gaza. He told no one about it.

Ten days later, Nir was critically injured in combat in northern Gaza. He was in a coma on life support fighting for his life for four months, during which he occasionally regained consciousness.

In the hospital, when his wife, Chen, asked him if he had written anything, he answered that he hadn't. "I think he just refused to let go," says Chen. "Even in the letter itself, he writes his parting words and in the same breath talks about our future together."

After he succumbed to his wounds, Chen didn't look for a letter. But she found it when scrolling by happenstance through his messages, a few days before the memorial service held a month after his death. Chen found the letter in his WhatsApp group with himself, which was meant for managing the business he had established. "Suddenly, among all the technical business messages, I noticed a message full of hearts and smileys. I felt as if he had written it to me just then, a message from the World to Come." During the memorial service, Chen read out parts of his letter.

We're Going to Enter the Gates of Life and Death

Nir Hadad

A letter to my loved ones ***as we go out to war.***

We're going to enter the gates of life and death.

Life that we want to give and bring to the world, death that the enemy longs for with all his heart.

Life that we want to increase and sense and feel.

Death that the enemy hungers for, because that is his sustenance.

To my heart's loves:

Chen, my dear love, my special one and only,

About six years ago, I got to meet you, and my life changed from then on.

I grew up, but I grew up together with you. I changed, but together with you. I matured, but together with you.

As we go out to war: Nir didn't actually receive an emergency call up to reserves. As the father of a daughter with complex medical needs, he was exempt from reserve duty.

"They say that the soldiers went out without thinking twice. But Nir thought a thousand times," says his wife, Chen. "He knew how much the twins and I need him; also, the business he dreamed of, to be a financial advisor for young couples, was just starting to take off."

Even so, Nir volunteered for reserve duty as a tank driver. When he left for his second

You were my anchor, my home, my deep bond and embrace so that I always knew there was a place for me. I'm happy for those six years – for each and every moment of them.... I love you and wish us many many many years together – **more than 120** *in health and unending love. I know that you hold me in very high regard but it's important to me that you know and always remember – it's largely thanks to you, and more than that – you're an outstanding role model yourself. The person that you are, the mother that you are, the partner that you are, the teacher that you are, and the woman that you are in the world.*

The goodness and the warmth that you give over to the world is wonderful and heartwarming.

Roni – little Bonbon – my firstborn daughter (by only two minutes but there's nothing to do about it, Noga...)

I learn a lot from you. I enjoy being with you even more. I learn about you and about myself and about the world every day – much of it thanks to you. What strength is, what joy is, and so many other things that children like you can teach us – the grown-ups.

Thank you for each and every moment with you and I so hope for many more moments like these – for long, healthy, good years together.

I love you with all my heart.

round of reserve duty and went into Gaza, he said to Chen, "Wow, it's really not right for me right now, with the girls at home and the business and everything. But I saw the video of the surveillance soldiers' kidnapping I simply can't stay home."

More than 120: Jews traditionally wish each other to live to 120 years, Moses's lifespan (Deut. 34:7).

***Cookies**, beautiful Noga –*

My love for you is endless.

You're a wise, understanding girl with exceptional emotional depth. We've felt that more than once even though you're still such a little girl.

Sensitivity, paying attention, and love represent you.

If only I would have many more long years with you, to learn you, to get to know you, and to get closer and closer.

I love you so so much.

Mommy –

*In a certain sense, **you were alone for so many years** and you raised a glorious family. We always said that like a cliché, but I believe it with all my heart.*

Six kids, each one more challenging than the next (except for the third; he was easy…).

I received so much from you and much of what I am today is thanks to your guidance, your education, the goodness you gave over to us at home, the positivity and optimism even in impossible situations.

You always knew how to go on, to be there for us, and I hope that you also knew how to pay attention to yourself. I hope.

Hopefully you're happy with us, you see value in us, you see us as a success among your actions, and in your life.

To many more long years filled with goodness.

Cookies: Noga and Roni were four-year-old twins. Nir came up with the nickname "Cookies," Ugiyot, for Noga based on her name – it evolved from Noga to Nugi, and then to Ugi, and from that to Ugiyot.

You were alone for so many years: When Nir was seven, his father passed away. Nir always admired his mother, Tzviya, for her personality, her choice to keep living, and for raising six children on her own, including a daughter with special needs.

My dear siblings –

Yaniv, Shimrita, Avrum, Elad, and Tzuf.

Five siblings, each one more special than the next.

***Yaniv** – True we're a little distant, but at every stage I've had tremendous appreciation for you and learned a lot from you. Thank you.*

***Shimrita** – I love you so much, Roni and Noga's favorite aunt; you're all heart and great love – may everything be good for you.*

***Avrum** – Keep up the good that you bring to the world. As a person, an employee, a coworker, a partner, a father, and a person in the world. Your goodness is felt and gladdens the heart. And your sense of responsibility… there's so much to learn from you.*

***Elad** – Beloved brother. Four and a half years older than me – I always felt like that, too… so close in age but also emotionally close. Your heart is wide and full of concern and love. Roni and Noga's favorite uncle, and you earned it fair.*

***Tzuftzuf** – You're still young, with a long life yet ahead of you – make the right choices, be happy with life, make others happy, do good, and may you be granted a good and happy life. I hope that I was, at the very least, a nice older brother…. I know I wasn't the ideal, definitely during our teenage years… but I wanted to be good.*

*To my sisters-in-law, **Racheli** and **Elisheva,***

I love you so much; keep up the good work for the sake of our shared, unified, big, special family. Love you lots and appreciate every step.

To the world – do good, make more good.

Make more great love, positivity, perfection, hard work, achievements, challenges; challenge yourselves, take on responsibilities, find out what you're good at and give it to the world – the world has a long way to go…

But don't forget –

There's evil in the world. There's pure evil that we have an obligation to overthrow and to destroy.

For this we go out to war, today – to overthrow this dirty, bad, hateful, and bloodthirsty evil. The kind of evil that's been attacking the Jews in every generation for thousands of years and exists out there in the world.

***The Jewish people never go away** and have the power to come back to life like the phoenix, each time stronger and more beautiful.*

May we know better days,

And I hope this whole thing will never become known…

ולואי וכל הדבר הזה לא יתפרסם לעולם...

The Jewish people never go away: "This language of pathos? It's not like him," says his wife, Chen. "They raised us in a youth movement on people like Roi Klein [who saved lives by jumping on a grenade before it detonated], but Nir wasn't that dramatic. He lived like that, but he didn't talk like that. I'm dying to meet him for a moment to ask him what he was feeling at that moment when he wrote the letter."

Adi Leon

Staff Sergeant Adi Leon, from Nili, served in the Tzabar Battalion, Givati Brigade. He fell in combat in the Namer [Tiger] APC disaster in the northern Gaza Strip on 16 Heshvan 5784/October 31, 2023. He is survived by his parents and two sisters. He was twenty when he fell.

Adi wrote his last letter in a notebook before entering Gaza for the first time, presumably on October 20, 2023. On its cover he wrote:

"To be read in the event of my death.

Adi Leon

Tzabar, Givati, Rifleman."

Before going into Gaza, Adi left the notebook in the safekeeping of Raz, his deputy company sergeant major, and said, "I hope to return and tear it up, but if, God forbid, anything happens to me – give it to my parents."

Adi was killed a week later, and Raz indeed passed the notebook along to Adi's family.

Adi was a part of a twelve-man team, of which eleven were killed together in what became known as the "APC tragedy." An anti-tank missile hit their armored personnel carrier, causing a powerful explosion that killed all the soldiers inside except for the driver.

Aside from Adi's letter, this book also includes last letters written by some of his friends who were killed along with him: Itay Yehuda, Roi Dawi, Erez Mishlovsky, Shay Arvos, and Adi Danan.

I Hope You Remember Me

Adi Leon

I never thought I would ever have to write something like this. I tried to put it off again and again, but they told us that we're going into Gaza tomorrow and there is a possibility that we may not come back, there are a few things I need you to know before it's over.

Dear Mom and Dad,

Although I don't show you that much love or spend a lot of time with you, I want you to know how much I appreciate you. Even when I was having a tough time, you never wavered in your efforts to get close to me and help me. Even when I spoke to you disrespectfully and gave up on everything, you never gave up on me.

You always made sure that we had everything – that we lacked for nothing. You work very hard for that. We had such a wonderful upbringing, and that was something I started to understand and appreciate more when Zohar grew up. Lately, I've almost never been at home, and even when I was, my mind was elsewhere. I'm really, really sorry for that – for not spending more time with my family, and for thinking only about having a good time. In the end, family is everything, and you always accepted me the way I am. You mean everything to me.♡

Zohar, my amazing sister ♡

As I write this, I look back at all our moments together as children – how much fun we had together and how we would always be looking for things to do, how we would get up before our parents in the morning and make them breakfast, how we filmed funny clips and pretended to be famous; how we would constantly drive Ori crazy and we couldn't stop laughing until our sides split.

We're both grown up now, and each of us is absorbed in our own pursuits, you in your room and I at parties. I really miss my childhood with you.

Now you are the elder sister in the family. It's a tough task, but I'm sure you'll be up to it, because that's who you are: responsible, wise, and caring – some might say "the successful sister."

I love you so much, and it's important to me that you remember that. I'm sorry I can't tell you that in person ♡

Oriki, my little sister, I don't think that God could create anything sweeter and more perfect than you. I'm writing this after not seeing you for two weeks, and it feels like eternity. I wish I could hug you one last time.

You're only 10 years old, and still so innocent. I always enjoy seeing you get excited and enthusiastic discovering new things. It reminds me of myself. Sometimes I even envy you.

I don't know how a girl your age is supposed to read something like this or how you will accept it, but always remember that I love you and miss you.

And if you want you can always talk to me in your thoughts. I'll be listening to you, even from Heaven above ♡

Cat doodle: At the end of his message to Ori, Adi drew a cat.

"We're a house with cats; we have four of them at home," his mother, Nurit, explains. "Adi knew how much Ori loves cats and wanted to make her happy."

As he suggested, Ori continues to communicate with Adi in her thoughts. She says that he sends her signs.

I can't write to everyone because I've been privileged to meet so many people during my life, but it is nevertheless important to me to express my gratitude to you for all the you moments and experiences that you gave me.

To the Leon family and the Perlberg family: I have always felt at east with you. The warm and homey atmosphere, your generosity and humor always gave me the feeling that there was something in me from each and every one of you. I truly thank you for everything. I love you, and I regret every family dinner and event I did not attend, because I know that I missed out on amazing experiences and people.

To my good friends, both girls and guys: we truly had so many great adventures together that I can't even begin to list them all.

Thank you for always being there for me and making my childhood amazing. ***I hope you celebrate like we planned to after my return,*** *and that you tell your children about the moments and experiences we shared.*

I miss you with all my heart. ♡

I am heading into this war with the knowledge that I may not return, but I believe with all my heart in what I am doing.

I hope you celebrate like we planned to after my return: Adi loved parties and made electronic music.

His mother, Nurit, promised him: "When the war is over and all your soldier friends come back home, I'll close off the street in front of our house and throw you a royal feast, a street party like in the old days." After Adi was killed, his parents decided to fulfill his mother's promise. Friends from all over the country came to a huge party that she threw on what would have been Adi's twenty-first birthday. At the entrance, they hung a sign that read: "I hope you'll celebrate like we planned after my return."

We have no other country and now it's my turn to defend it *and avenge all the civilians, soldiers, babies, and old people, and all the women who were* ***helpless*** *against the atrocities of Hamas.*

This is what my parents taught me,
This is what I believe in,

I hope you will remember me,

מקווה שתזכרו אותי

Adi ♡ ✡

We have no other country and now it's my turn to defend it: When Adi came out of Kfar Aza on October 11 in the middle of the night, after a few straight days of combat, he called his parents and said: "I've seen sights that no one in the world should see."

Before his parents drove out to meet him in the Gaza Envelope, they asked him what he needed. Adi answered: "Get me a commando knife."

His mother was surprised and had no idea how to get ahold of a knife like that in the middle of the night. The only person she could think of that might have a commando knife was her father, who died a year before Adi was killed. He was a Holocaust survivor and used to say, "We know what happens to us when we don't have an army." And indeed, she found a commando knife in one of the compartments of her father's car, and brought it to Adi.

Adi made an attachment for it to his vest, and carried his grandfather's knife on him throughout his fighting in Gaza.

Helpless: In all of Adi's long goodbye letter, there is only one spelling error. Misspelling the Hebrew word for helpless to resemble something like "answer-less" is his only mistake. "Adi never had spelling mistakes," recounts his mother. "On October 7th, among the horrors that he saw in the Gaza Envelope, he saw people who were not only helpless but completely without anyone to respond to them, answer-less."

I hope that you'll remember me: President Isaac Herzog read the closing lines of Adi's letter on the Knesset podium and said:

"In my name and in the name of all citizens of the State of Israel, I promise Adi that we'll never forget."

Adi's letter has been set to music, translated into five languages, and incorporated into a lesson plan called "The Lights of Adi," which is studied in Israeli schools and in Jewish communities worldwide. Parents who didn't know Adi have named their children for him.

"A modest guy who made a modest request," says his mother. "He only said, 'I hope you remember me.' And a great many people have answered him."

Itay Yehuda

Staff Sergeant Itay Yehuda, from Rishon LeTzion, served in the Tzabar Battalion, Givati Brigade. He fell in combat in the APC disaster in the northern Gaza Strip on 16 Heshvan 5784/ October 31, 2023. He is survived by his parents and two siblings. He was twenty-one when he fell.

Itay wrote his last letter in a pocket notepad on October 27, 2023, mere minutes before the ground incursion into Gaza.

Four days later, Itay was killed in the APC disaster. The letter that he carried with him survived, burnt and covered in soot.

The family managed to decipher most of the words, but some of the text was completely burnt. Those parts are marked with brackets.

Thanks to You, I Never Stopped Laughing

Itay Yehuda

Friday, 6:41 pm. Where should I begin?

Who would have thought that I'd need to write a goodbye letter. To my parents, I want to say thank you for raising me and educating me to be who I am and ***where I've gotten to****. I appreciate you so much, even if it didn't always seem […]*

Omer and Adi […] the best […]

To the friends and people I knew over my life: thank you for all the moments that I had with you, for all the outings and laughter. ***Thanks to you, I never stopped laughing****. I love you like crazy. Aside from that, it's important to me to say that I don't regret enlisting for combat for a moment, and it's the best thing I've gone through in my life. If you're reading this letter, it's a sign that I completed […] in order to protect […]*

סיימתי את... בשביל להגן

Where I've gotten to: Itay studied art in high school and was a gifted artist. He dreamed of opening a studio and spent much of his short leaves from the army going to a painting class to develop his talents. A short time before he was killed in the *Namer* [Tiger] APC disaster, Itay drew a giant picture of a beautiful tiger. After his death, his work was displayed at various exhibitions, including his local municipality building.

Thanks to you, I never stopped laughing: Itay was always laughing. The APC driver, the sole survivor of the disaster in which Itay and ten of his friends were killed, witnessed the team's last moments. He shared that in their final drive together, Itay's infectious, captivating laughter spread to the entire team. They were all laughing from Itay's jokes until their last moment, when the anti-tank missile hit their vehicle.

Roi Dawi

Staff Sergeant Roi Dawi, from Jerusalem, squad commander in the Tzabar Battalion, Givati Brigade. He fell in combat in the APC disaster in the northern Gaza Strip on 16 Heshvan 5784/ October 31, 2023. He is survived by his parents, sister, brother, and a partner. He was twenty when he fell.

On October 7th, Roi rushed to the Gaza Envelope and waged intense battle in Kfar Aza for three days straight.

On October 9, 2023, he wrote his last letter and saved it in his personal WhatsApp group with himself to be opened only upon his death. He told a good friend and his partner Nitzan about the letter.

In a voice message that he sent to Nitzan right before he went into Gaza, he said: "I'm not going anywhere, really, I don't want you to think like that, that I'm about to die. It's not the right mindset! I'm going to go in, kill terrorists, and come back. This doesn't have to be the way we talk to each other, like it's our final conversation."

Two weeks later, Roi was killed in the APC disaster. Their talk about the letter turned out to be their final conversation.

If I'm to Die, Then Only Like This

Roi Dawi

Mom, Dad, Nitzani, Eden, and Tomer, I love you.

You were the best there is; ***if I'm to die then only like this.***

I hope we flatten Gaza before this reaches you.

I regret nothing. I had the best service I could ask for with the sweetest end there is.

My soldiers are lions; it's a privilege to command them.
Liel's pathway is with us here, too; the smile comes out

If I'm to die then only like this: "In both of Roi's swearing-in ceremonies – as a soldier and a commander – when he shouted the words 'and even to sacrifice my life,' he looked at me," says his mother, Betty. "He saw that I flinched, skipped a beat. We never spoke about that moment; we're not a home that talks about death. We didn't think Roi would be required to be tested over his vow. But when I read those words, 'If I'm to die, then only like this,' I felt that for the first time he was answering the question that I never dared to ask."

Liel's pathway is with us here, too; the smile comes out at every possible moment: The "Liel" Roi refers to here by first name, as if he was his good friend, is someone that Roi never met. Whoever knew Roi immediately knew that he was talking about Liel Gidoni, of blessed memory, a fighter from the Givati Infantry Brigade who was killed in Gaza in Operation Protective Edge (a series of Israeli airstrikes in 2014 in response to missiles fired at the south of the country from Gaza).

Roi was twelve years old when Liel Gidoni was killed. Roi learned about him and was inspired by him, and enlisted in Givati to follow in his footsteps. Both of them grew up in the same Jerusalem neighborhood, went to the same school, and were fans of the Hapoel Jerusalem basketball team. Both of them fell in Gaza at the age of twenty-one.

From the age of twelve until his death, Roi's Instagram bio was: "'Smile, because a smile is joy, and joy is the strength to carry on' (Staff Sergeant Liel Gidoni)."

at every possible moment. *To see* ***everyone who's here*** *– that's the Land of Israel, for whose sake I'm doing this.*

Let the people who don't want to serve, keep refusing reserve service; meanwhile we'll go into Gaza.

Nitzani, my love, you're my little angel. Thank you for the time with you and for everything you taught me. You're a champion; believe in yourself. Be strong for me. ***You'll be the best jeweler in the world.***

To my friends – thank you for being who you are. I am who I am thanks to you.

Mom and Dad, who don't want to drive me crazy so they don't call, you were everything I could have wished for myself and more. Promise me one thing – that Mom will keep going to ***Hapoel games*** *– but with you this time!*

Everyone who's here: Roi wrote this after three days of intense fighting in Kfar Aza. "Everyone who's here" at that point in time were the friends who fought at his side and the residents of the kibbutz that he managed to save.

A resident from Kfar Aza that his family had never met came to Roi's shiva. She told them that she recognized Roi's picture on the news after he was killed: This was the face that she saw on October 7th, when Roi came to rescue her and her children from their home's safe room.

You'll be the best jeweler in the world: As long as Roi had known Nitzan, her dream was to be a jeweler, and Roi always pushed her to believe in her potential and to turn her passion into her profession.

On October 4, three days before the war broke out, Roi took her to a few stores that sold metalwork equipment to encourage her to get started.

Roi's letter was published after his death. As a result, several art schools reached out to Nitzan and invited her to apply to their professional metalwork courses. Today she is studying at one of them and planning to establish a business.

Hapoel games: Roi was a huge fan of the Hapoel Jerusalem basketball team.

My beloved Eden and Tomer, there aren't many bonds like ours. You were my safe place for everything – exemplary, model older siblings.

Teach them how it's done, and just get stronger from it all.

Dawi

תעשו לכולם בית ספר ורק תתחזקו מהכל.

דאוי

Erez Mishlovsky

Staff Sergeant Erez Mishlovsky, from Oranit, served in the Tzabar Battalion, Givati Brigade. He fell in combat in the *Namer* (APC) disaster in the northern Gaza Strip on 16 Heshvan 5784/ October 31, 2023. He is survived by his parents, a brother, two sisters, and a partner. He was twenty when he fell.

Erez wrote his last letter in his private notebook the night before the first ground incursion into Gaza.

Four days later, Erez fell in the APC (Armored Personnel Carrier) disaster. The notebook he kept on him was found completely burned on the outside, but the words inside it survived.

If So, Then So

Erez Mishlovsky

Hi,

I had so many things I wanted to write, but at the moment of truth everything just slips out of my head. Who would have believed the day would come when I'd be entering Gaza as a fighter. I always thought I'd come up with some good catchphrase of my own, something a bit cynical but meaningful. I think I'll go with: Im kvar az kvar – "(If so) If I'm already going in, (then so) then it's all the way." ***Feels like the right phrase; hopefully it will catch on.***

In my opinion this phrase carries a positive meaning. You can take it in many directions, like: "(If so) If going in, (then so) then let it be interesting," or "(If so) If I'm a fighter, (then so) then it should be a fighter in Givati."

Just kidding…

If so, then so – I chose this catchphrase because I think the best way to complete it is: "(If so) If I'm already going in, (then so) then it's for my family, my friends, and my people." In the end, when I was a child, others always protected me. Now it's my turn to protect you. This feels like the right way.

Now for the hard part.

Feels like the right phrase; hopefully it will catch on : Erez's family engraved the words "If I'm already in, then it's all in" on his tombstone. Now Erez's sentence is all over the country, printed on T-shirts, bumper stickers, and posters.

Dear Mom and Dad, I want you to know that I always love you. Even when we had our little arguments, I know it always came from a place of caring. ***I want you to know that I appreciate everything you've done for me*** *and the support you've given me. It's not something that I take for granted.*

Guy, Aayah, and Noa, I want to thank you for everything. For silly fights we had, the laughs we always shared, the impressions we used to do of one another, in short for everything we did together. Know that I love you and appreciate everything you've done for me.

Dear family and friends, thank you for all the support you've given me. I love you and appreciate you from the bottom of my heart. Thank you for being part of my life. I love you,

Erez

"If so, then so"

I want you to know that I appreciate everything you've done for me: "You raise the kids, teach them and hope to impart values to them, but you don't really know how much of this actually gets absorbed," says Sophie, Erez's mother. "And suddenly you read the letter and discover that it's all inside. All the insights of his whole life are just right there."

Eden, my monster,

I don't even know where to begin. We've been through such a long, fun, and joyful journey, or, as you said, a meaningful one. We're about to reach a year together. Babe, who would have thought more than eight months have already gone by? This time with you has been the best period of my life. I've learned so much, and I've enjoyed being with you so deeply. As I'm writing this, I realize just how much I love you, ***my life****. My darling, my beauty, my monster, my only one,* ***my life****.*

I always knew I had a lot to say, but when it comes down to it, it's the hardest. But since you know me so well, I'm sure you already know how I feel about you. My love, I love you and I always will, no matter what. You'll always be in my heart.
I love you, my monster.

"אם כבר אז כבר"

Eden, my monster: When Erez and his siblings were little, their mother Sophie would affectionately call them "my monsters." When Erez fell in love with his partner Eden, he adopted that nickname for her. After Erez fell, one way Eden memorialized him was through the round, green monster character Mike Wazowski from the movie *Monsters, Inc.*

My life: *Chayim Sheli*, a common Israeli term of endearment for loved ones.

The Gratitude of a Freed Hostage

Emily Damari

During my days in captivity, when the cries of "Bring them home" echoed through every corner, I knew that a whole country would not abandon its children.

I knew that there were soldiers – male and female – risking their lives to bring us home. But only after I came back did I understand the terrible price paid by too many.

Today, when I look bereaved families in the eye, I see the tremendous pain of that loss.

All of us – me, but mostly the families who lost those most dear to them – have borne the heaviest price of this war. There are no words that can comfort the bereaved, but there are words that can commemorate the fallen.

This book is more than a collection of their letters. It is a living testament to their strong and not-to-be-taken-for-granted love for country, for family, and for life itself. This book allows us to hear their voices, to sense their dreams, to touch the elevated qualities of their souls. Each letter preserves a memory that must not be forgotten.

I think of the words that Aviad Nayman of blessed memory wrote in his last letter. Aviad made it out of Gaza safely, and then fell in combat in Lebanon:

Take life easy. Everything is small, everything is transient, but everything matters so much. Pay attention to the little details that most people miss. To the friend who's looking for help and feels uncomfortable asking or the neighbor who writes a vague message on WhatsApp and actually needs help and support.

Aviad's words bring me back to my relationship with Gali and Ziv Berman,[1] who were taken captive with me into Gaza.

I had the privilege of having my good friends as neighbors, and together we built a relationship based on mutual support, concern, and assistance – the kind where, in any situation and for any need, you show up for each other.

To my regret, this neighborliness led us to a shared fate, when on the morning of the Black Shabbat, Gali showed up when I asked. And moments later, they took us both captive to Gaza, with Zivi close behind.

And here I am now, free. Thanks to the bereaved families. Thanks to the heroes of this book.

Thanks to their courage, self-sacrifice, and determination.

And as I go on with my life, every day I carry with me the responsibility to live a life of meaning, for my sake and for theirs. We will remember them not just in our grief, but in our actions, in our joys, and in continuing to make life. This is their true legacy – that we continue onward, build a better world, and carry on their memory with pride and with love.

1. Gali and Ziv Berman are twin brothers who returned to Israel in the hostage deal on October 13, 2025 after being in captivity for two years. They were separated the day they were taken hostage and were reunited for the first time on the day of their release.

Shay Arvas

Staff Sergeant Shay Arvas, from Holon, combat medic in the Tzabar Battalion, Givati Brigade. He fell in combat in the APC disaster in the northern Gaza Strip on 16 Heshvan 5784/ October 31, 2023. He is survived by his parents, four siblings, and a partner. He was twenty when he fell.

On October 19, 2023, before entering Gaza, Shay wrote his last letter in the Notes app on his phone. A week and a half later, he was killed in the APC disaster.

After his death, his family received his phone and found his letter, entitled "In the Event That…".

Grandfather, Be Proud Now, Too, Because I Didn't Fall in Vain

Shay Arvas

In the event that...

To my beloved Adar, to my dear mom, to the best dad in the world, and all my siblings, Chen and Tami, Ray and Imri, Or and Niv, Ran and Moriya, Emily and Ari and Tal and Stav, and the close family,

You should know how much I miss you and I love you, and the truth is that I was happy to do what I'm doing, ***to save people and protect the country, because that's something I always wanted.*** *Something that was always a part of me, ever since I was little, and now I had the opportunity to do it and give of myself to the country.*

So you should know that all this wasn't in vain and it was worth it. For all of Am Yisrael to continue this tradition. And to love the country, because people didn't fall here for nothing, ***and there are people here that we need to protect.***

To save people and protect the country, because that's something I always wanted: In high school, motivated by his dream to save lives, Shay volunteered for the Israeli ambulance service Magen David Adom, through which he met his partner Adar, during Covid, when both of them volunteered to babysit for the children of physicians.

When he enlisted, aside from being a fighter in the lead company of the battalion, he volunteered to take a combat medic course. On October 7th, during the fierce battles in Kfar Aza, Shay and his fellow soldiers saved the lives of 102 civilians.

And there are people here that we need to protect: A week before Shay was killed, his brother Ran had a baby boy. Ran sent Shay a photo of his new nephew, whom Shay

I know that it'll be hard but I want for you to keep going how you are. Keep on living, ***give as much of yourselves as you can,*** *be a unified family.*

Adar, my love, keep on doing your thing. It'll be hard, but I really want for you to be as happy as you are now, and for you to move on.

And all my close friends, I love you and appreciate you for all the life and experiences we went through together. It was fun, I enjoyed it a lot, and I had a happy life. ***Grandpa, I know that you always believed in me and you were very proud of me becoming a fighter,***

So be proud now, too, because I didn't fall in vain

אז תהיה גאה גם עכשיו,
כי לא נפלתי לחינם

had never met, and Shay wrote back: "I'm really happy! This is why I stayed to protect you." Soon after Shay's death, his brother Tal also had his first child, a daughter they named for him, Shay-Li.

Give as much of yourselves as you can: During high school, Shay would regularly visit a Holocaust survivor named Aviva Ben Yakar. After his death, she said:

"Even though we were sixty years apart, Shay and I clicked and became friends. He's a wonderful young man! He would visit me regularly and we would laugh together, drink coffee, and eat cake. He even brought me cakes that he had baked himself. Once he rode over to me on his bike to bring me a big, beautiful cake he baked in honor of my seventy-fifth birthday. It's difficult for me to describe how much that touched me. He had a photo of the two of us printed on the cake with the dedication 'Happy Birthday, My Queen!'

"Even after Shay enlisted in the army, he kept visiting me. He came in uniform. I gave him a big hug and asked God to watch over him."

Grandpa, I know that you always believed in me and you were very proud of me becoming a fighter: Yaakov, Shay's grandfather, fought in the Yom Kippur and in the First Lebanon Wars. "Because I was a fighter myself, Shai and I would converse a lot about combat service," says Grandpa Yaakov. "I would ask him how training was, how it was on the line, what he experienced. He was moved to see how interested I was. He was proud that he carried on the tradition."

Adi Danan

Staff Sergeant Adi Danan, from Yavneh, squad commander in the Tzabar Battalion, Givati Brigade. He fell in combat in the APC disaster in the northern Gaza Strip on 16 Heshvan 5784/October 31, 2023. He is survived by his parents, two sisters, and a partner. He was twenty when he fell.

In a phone call between Adi and his partner Yahli the evening before going into Gaza, he told her: "Roi Dawi, the sergeant, and other guys here are writing letters to their family. I don't get it. They don't understand that we're coming back?"

Yahli reassured him and said to him that he didn't have to write. "We know how much you love us; you don't have to add anything more."

Nevertheless, Adi decided to leave a letter. He wrote it in the Notes app on his phone on October 26, 2023, and called his close friend Dvir.

They spoke about the imminent entrance into Gaza, and Adi told him about all the horrors that he saw in Kfar Aza on October 7th, from which he returned a different person. At the end of the conversation, Adi said to him, "I'm sending you a letter; you're my best friend and I trust you not to read it. If something happens to me, support my family, and stay by my partner's side and look out for her."

A week later, on October 31, 2023, Adi was killed with ten other soldiers in the northern Gaza Strip when the *Namer* [Tiger] APC [Armored Personnel Carrier] of the Tzabar Battalion in the Givati Brigade was struck by an anti-tank missile. A malfunction in the system designed to provide active protection for the vehicle prevented interception of the strike, resulting in the destruction of the vehicle and the soldiers' deaths. The incident is considered one of the most tragic disasters to have struck the Givati Brigade during the war, leaving a heavy mark on the families, the brigade, and the entire system.

These are the names of the soldiers that were killed: Sergeant Adi Danon, Staff Sergeant Itay Yehuda, Staff Sergeant Shay Arvas, Staff Sergeant Hillel Solomon, Staff Sergeant Erez Mishlovsky, Staff Sergeant Adi Leon, Corporal Ido Ovadia, Corporal Lior Siminovich, Staff Sergeant Roi Dawi, Second Lieutenant Mark Pedya.

As soon as Dvir heard the news, he drove to Adi's home and handed his family the letter.

In Case Something Happens to Me, I Have Something to Tell You

Adi Danan

My family,

I know that in the end, this might just be a letter to myself, that everything will be okay and the war will be over, but in the end, in case something happens to me, I have something to tell you before I go in.

I can tell you that I was granted the best family I could have asked for. You turned me into an independent kid who knows how to respect his parents and appreciate everything I have, you taught me to appreciate mankind and everyone around me, and to speak, to consider what's good and what isn't good.

You never let me lack for anything; everything that I wanted, I had, and for this I thank you.

Dad: I know you'll tell me I'm being an idiot and what are you writing things like this for, but in the end I don't get to decide what will happen in there and what won't. But I'll be the world's most careful person in everything I do.

I got to have you, the best friend, my confidant, the person I admire, the man who watches over me. You always looked out for me, you were always there even when I didn't need it, you always showed fatherly concern and endless love.

I love you on a level that you couldn't even fathom, but I ask a personal favor of you: Take care of the family, be there for whoever needs it, show them a smile, and raise this family up, because you're its heart.

Mom: My queen, the woman I love most in the world. I don't have many words to say aside from thank you. Thank you for looking out for me, for raising me, for accepting me, for being there for me, for getting excited and for getting annoyed.

In the end, I can tell you that you made me what I was, the best creation someone could possibly make.

I want you to know that I just love you to a degree that you don't even fathom, and I ask – please take care of everyone and be strong. I want you to know that you're the person who touches me the most; I love you forever.

My sisters.

My twin, ***flesh of my flesh****, the person who understands me the best in the whole world. I don't even know how to begin, but I will say that I love you, Linoya, and even if something happens I'll always be there for you and take care of you from above.*

You're my twin sister, the person I've experienced every moment with since we were cute little babies and ***until we grew up and became soldiers****. I love you, my Linoya, and I will love you forever.*

Flesh of my flesh: A reference to Genesis 2:23.

Until we grew up and became soldiers: "After Adi fell, I took his purple beret and put it on me," says his twin sister, Linoy. "I wear it all over the country and tell about him, so that they'll remember my Adidi, always and everywhere."

Little Liori, the one I've watched over for life.

I still remember when we were in fourth grade and me and Linoy were lying in Mom and Dad's bed when we were little, and they brought you, this fat creature, to the bed and told us this is your sister. From that moment, I knew that I'd watch over you for life.

You made me the happiest brother in the world, I love you so much. Keep being that smiley girl who loves everyone, and I ask you to do our parents proud, be a good girl Liori, invest in your studies because I want to hear that you have some good college degree that'll help you in life, and ultimately be a good person, because I'm here all the time, watching over you from above. I love you forever.

My Yahli: ***My own Chinese girl****, the person who really made me know what it is to love and how to be in love.*

I remember that we got to know each other in ***Michveh Alon*** *in between shifts on guard, and you weren't in dating mode at all, but I still remember our click in those first conversations, that small connection that gave me butterflies in my stomach, the smile that would come to my face every time I get a message from you or wait for a phone call, whenever I could.*

My own Chinese girl: Yahli, Adi's partner, has slightly slanted eyes, and that's what Adi would affectionately call her. Adi and Yahli met on Instagram while Adi was posted at the Michveh Alon base, and before they met in person they would spend hours on the phone to pass his long guard hours. Yahli says that even though they had only been together for five months, Adi would tell her every evening that their love was forever.

After Adi fell, Yahli decided to enlist in the Givati Brigade where he had served.

Michveh Alon: An IDF training base near Safed known for integrating non-native Hebrew speakers into the IDF.

You made me love, my Yahli; you made me feel safe to know how to open up as needed and how to show your boundless love.

Maybe we've only been together for five months, but it feels to me like we've already been together for years.

I ask you, my Yahli, I'm with you and I'm here for life. **How does Yonatan Kalimi say it:** *"I'm here even if nothing works out," so I'm really here, even from above, watching you all the time, loving you with endless love, my woman, and I'll keep on loving you all the time.*

Thank you for being part of me and making me know that I was granted the best thing I could have asked for. I love you, my Babu.

Additionally, I want to say thank you to all my friends and all the people who've been at my side my whole life. You made me who I am and you brought out my joy for life; I love you.

My family and my Yahli, you're everything to me and I'll always love you.

Thank you for being part of me

תודה שהייתם חלק ממני

How does Yonatan Kalimi say it: Adi would often quote this line from a song by his favorite singer, Yonatan Kalimi: "I'm here even if nothing works out." Yonatan came to Adi's funeral, and after learning more about him, he released the song "Don't Worry, Mom," based on Adi's letter.

Mark Kononovich

Sergeant Major (Reserves) Mark Kononovich, from Herzliya, served in the 8208 Battalion, 261st Brigade. He fell in combat in the southern Gaza Strip on 12 Shevat 5784/ January 22, 2024. He is survived by his wife, four children, parents, and two siblings. He was thirty-five when he fell.

When Mark left his home to fight on October 7th, his wife, Orel, pleaded with him to leave a letter behind. "Look at our children," she said to him. "She's a week old and he's two. If something happens to you, they won't remember you. What will I be able to show them?"

Mark refused. He insisted that he'd come back safely and he didn't want to say goodbye.

On January 22, at two in the morning, he wrote his last letter in the Notes app on his phone. Just a few hours later, Mark fell in combat together with twenty other soldiers.

When his wife received his phone during the shiva, she was surprised to find his letter: "When I asked him to write, I thought he'd write something more like the typical letter: that he'd say goodbye, I love you, grow up, laugh – all the usual things they say to kids. Instead, he wrote something completely different. But then I understood: Mark really didn't need to say that he loved us. That's what he fought for; that's why he went out to fight on October 7th. That was a given."

You'll Suddenly Realize That You're Not Eternal

Mark Kononovich

One day, a sun-drenched morning or a late, rainy evening.

You'll suddenly realize that ***everything will happen to you when it needs to happen****. And the people who are with you aren't eternal, and the fact is that neither are you.*

You'll realize that it's all meaningless; you're using up your time the wrong way. You dream of something that will never happen. You're sad about something that cannot be fixed. You realize how many words you threw to the wind and how many words you took close to your heart.

You'll realize how many strangers passed through your life, as if through a corridor, and how many people close to your heart you didn't pay attention to because of your own stupidity. You'll realize that you need to change. There's no need to take everything to heart; don't expect a thing; ***don't be sorry over anything****.*

Everything will happen to you when it needs to happen: On October 7th, Mark's wife, Orel, stood at the door and asked him not to go out and fight.

Orel had lost her mother a year earlier and couldn't bear the thought of losing Mark as well.

"Look what they've done to us," Mark answered her, "The country has collapsed; there are two hundred hostages. I can't stay home."

After three months of fighting, when some of the reservists were released home, Orel asked Mark to come back home. He insisted that he wouldn't come back until the hostages were home. "How can I sleep in my own bed while they're sleeping in tunnels?"

Don't be sorry over anything: Two weeks before he was killed, Mark sent a message to his father for no apparent reason:

What needs to come – will come; what happened – there's no way to change.

In addition to the letter he wrote in Hebrew, Mark wrote up various quotes he'd gathered, in Russian; from a range of sources, from a Tibetan philosopher to a character in a video game:

"We keep the memory of exalted acts even when the image has faded from our memory. The memory remains even when they steal all the rest from us."

"A normal person doesn't wake up with the thought that today is the last day of his life. But I think that this is a privilege, not a curse. The knowledge that death is near grants freedom. This is the time for introspection. The enemy is strong, we're few, we're on the edge, marching toward certain death, but the sand and stones that have seen thousands of years of war, that have soaked up so much blood, will remember us. For we have chosen our path, and believe me, this path is more frightening than any nightmare. We have no other path; we have to do this. We will destroy evil."

"Keep your soul from all baseness, even if it leads you to the goal you aimed for, for you will find no replacement for a lost soul."

"There's a sort of desire to end life with honor. . . not to leave any debts behind me, so that my conscience won't nag at me if I hurt someone I love and didn't get to ask their forgiveness.

In general, there are so many things I want to do properly, fairly, and honestly."

His father, Alex, replied: "Your whole life is ahead of you, Mark! I'm proud of you; we're all proud of you. You don't owe anyone anything; you're paying your military debt to the country with integrity and honor for all of us! You love your children – protect them, that's the most proper, fair, and honest thing. We love you with all our heart and soul, we're worried and waiting for you to come back home. We're waiting for you, dear, beloved son."

"To understand ephemerality and death – means to understand that nothing lasts forever; all is fleeting as a dream."

"A tender mist wreathed the peaks of sadness."

"What a tremendous chasm exists between the dead, who revive your heart when you recall them, and the living, who kill your heart when you meet them."

"If only everyone would have something much more important than money."

"How far shall we go? – The question isn't how far. The question is how strong you are, how deep your faith is, to go as far as needed."

"The loving eyes of a mother… gaze at them for as long as they are not only a memory."

מה שצריך לבוא - יבוא, מה שקרה - אין דרך לשנות

Daniel Toaff

Captain Daniel Mimon Toaff, from Moreshet, deputy company commander of the Shaked Battalion, Givati Brigade. He died in combat in the southern Gaza Strip on 14 Elul 5784/September 17, 2024. He is survived by his parents and four siblings. He was twenty-three when he died.

Daniel wrote these words on October 27, 2023, before the beginning of the ground operations in Gaza.

He sent the letter to his good friend Keshet, and wrote: "Whoa. I just wrote down what I'm going to tell my soldiers before we go in, and something else for my family. How exciting this is. You can't fathom it. I swear, my whole life I haven't felt this exhilarated."

The next day, Daniel read his words to his soldiers as they stood together in a single cluster after weeks of training, ready to go into Gaza.

Even though Daniel was addressing a large group of soldiers, he still chose to read out even the personal words for his family, who received the letter a day after his funeral.

See What an Empire You Raised

Daniel Toaff

I'll begin with this: I remember when I was a child Grandma and Grandpa always used to say that when I grow up there won't be any more wars and they won't need an army. Very soon, I realized that this was incorrect, because I learned about Am Yisrael, the Land of Israel, and the State of Israel, that ***in every generation they stand against us to destroy us and the Holy One, blessed be He, saves us.***

We find ourselves at a historic moment, a moment that will be remembered for generations, and we here have been privileged to take part in that history. Another chapter in the story of the Jewish people.

Every chapter in the story of the Jewish people always begins with one thing – that is, internal strife among the people, when we dare to let it cross our minds that even someone who just thinks differently from us is disreputable and crazy and not part of the people; not part of us, simply out of touch.

When crises amidst the people arise, they always lead to national disaster like the one that happened to us just now – babies were slaughtered, whole families were cut

In every generation they stand against us to destroy us and the Holy One, blessed be He, saves us: A quotation from the Haggada, recited annually at the Passover Seder.

down, and we are left here in IDF uniform, obligated to protect our people, and ***we failed****. We have to say the truth.*

Now it's our turn, our turn to be those who bear the burden and take responsibility for the people. Like Abraham, Isaac, and Jacob, each one in his own trial; Moses, who brought the people up to the land; Joshua son of Nun, who conquered the land; David, Solomon, and the kings of Israel; Esther and Mordechai, the Maccabees, the ***underground resistance****, the partisans, the Jews of the Holocaust, IDF soldiers throughout the generations – they all took responsibility for their people. Now it's our turn.*

A month and a half ago was Rosh HaShana, the Ten Days of Repentance, and Yom Kippur. We all prayed for the collective, and I personally – the thing I always try to have in mind is to be inscribed in the Book of Good Life. The point here isn't to just live for another year and not die; the intent here is that we should have a life of meaning and doing good for the people of Israel and the Land of Israel.

We failed: On October 7th, Daniel held the line in Samaria, yet he still considered himself to have had a part in the IDF's failure to protect the Gaza Envelope. His soldiers say that Daniel was always alert as a commanding officer, and even in calmer times took care to be in peak preparedness for the possibility of war. On October 7th, Daniel and his platoon were the first of his battalion to reach the Gaza Envelope. Even after eleven straight months of fighting, Daniel ended his last phone call with his father with the words: "That's what we're here for. To the end, as much as is needed."

Underground resistance: Jewish forces during the British Mandate. Forerunners to the IDF.

I always try to keep this most in mind, asking for us to have a life of action for the sake of Am Yisrael, the Land of Israel, and the Torah of Israel. A life in which I make the world a better place, my people better. This is the purpose of life, and here I have reached the moment – and I have been privileged to enact this and to live this life, a life for the collective and doing good for the people of Israel, ***with my entire being.***

Thank you for the amazing, uncompromising education, with the eternal values of the eternal people who will eternally prevail. To my dear brothers and sister, I love you all. I have learned from you all; I'm always proud to recount what you do. You are my pride. Even if sometimes I act like a crazy kid, know that I always love you and am proud of you.

Thank you, Dad and Mom. My whole life you gave me everything I needed, but never let me get full of myself and think that the world exists for me. My whole life I've seen how you ***aim to do good wherever you are.*** *Whether it's Mom, who works day and night and is always worrying about the problems of our people wherever she is, how she never stands as a bystander but demands that truth and justice come to light. Or whether it's Dad, who works all the time for the people, for the*

With my entire being: After the fact, his family discovered that in one military action, Daniel got injured in the shoulder. He refused to be evacuated, treated his wound himself, and continued to fight with a wounded shoulder, without saying a word.

Aim to do good wherever you are: Daniel's mother Orit is a public interest lawyer who has spent her entire career fighting for justice. His father, Shlomo, is an executive vice president and head of the Air Defense Systems Division in Rafael Advanced Defense Systems, Ltd. Daniel was extremely proud of his parents and spoke about them at every opportunity, including in this speech that he gave his soldiers before entering Gaza for the first time.

defense and security of our people, and enjoys doing it in an inspiring way. You are the source of my life.

A person is formed by the landscape of his homeland; the landscape I grew up on is one of endless giving and doing for our people and nation, and not just looking out for my own self individually.

I love you and I demand of you: As long as I'm out there to fight evil and restore good for Am Yisrael – you be there at home, continuing to do good for our people. Never stop. Always keep your head held high and your chest swollen with pride because you succeeded. You succeeded in raising a faithful, generation devoted to the people of Israel, the Land of Israel, and the Torah of Israel.

See what an empire you raised, each child and his unique contribution to Am Yisrael. This is proof of good parents' success. Everyone should envy you that you succeeded in this way.

***May I merit to raise children and grandchildren** who are wise and understanding, who love the Lord and fear God, people of truth, holy seed who cling to God and light up the world with Torah and good deeds, and all works of the Creator.*

May I merit to raise children and grandchildren: These words of prayer are traditionally recited when lighting Shabbat candles on Friday night.

That's what you have succeeded in doing, and I pray that I will succeed as you have. ***We'll meet soon****; I ask you always to keep smiling, no matter what happens, and continue to act for the sake of the people and the land.*

I love you endlessly.

אוהב אתכם בלי סוף

We'll meet soon: Even though his speech is written as a goodbye letter, with a request to his parents to "keep smiling no matter what," Daniel writes that "we'll meet soon." One of the commanders who was present when Daniel read this part shares that, at the end of the speech, Daniel said to his soldiers, "Call your parents and tell them how happy you are, even if you're scared. Don't stress them out; you won't benefit from that – neither you nor them. Convey to them the great spirit that is with us here."

Kamay Achiel

Sergeant Kamay Achiel, from Rosh HaAyin, served in Navy Fleet 914, the Snapir Port Security Unit. She fell in combat on the northern border on 29 Tishrei 5784/ October 14, 2023. She is survived by her parents, two sisters, and a partner. She was eighteen when she fell.

At the beginning of the war, Kamay served on the Lebanon border as a combat solider in the Navy's Snapir [literally, "fin"] commando unit.

On October 11, moments after an anti-tank missile attack up north, Kamay spoke to her mother. When the conversation ended, Kamay wrote her last letter in the Notes app on her phone, and didn't tell anyone about it.

Three days later, she fell in combat.

When her family was looking through her phone for photos after her death, they happened to find the note with her last letter.

I Want You to Know That There's No One Happier Than I Am

Kamay Achiel

To my family, to ***my boyfriend****, to my close friends, I'm here at the Lebanon border doing my duty!* ***Protecting my country****, those most important to me.*

I'm writing this between sirens

Between going out to the border and returning to the outpost.

I want you to know that there's no one happier than I am that I chose to do what I'm doing.

I'm happy to get up every morning and serve my country in the Snapir Unit.

I love you. I pray and ask that all the hostages, all the missing, the families from north to south, stay safe and sound.

May all the IDF soldiers go in peace and return in peace!

We're the Chosen People

אנחנו העם הנבחר

My boyfriend: At the end of high school, Kamay started dating Nitai. An outstanding athlete, he received an exemption from the army to pursue an athletic career, but Kamay made a condition: If you want to be my boyfriend, you have to enlist and become a combat soldier. Nitai joined the paratroopers. Half a year after Kamay was killed he was badly wounded in battle in the Gaza Strip.

Protecting my country: Kamay was killed during an operation on the Lebanese border to thwart a terrorist attempt to invade via the sea.

Kamay took out a grenade and prepared to throw it onto the water to hit the terrorist divers underwater, but the grenade was faulty and exploded too early, killing Kamay on the spot.

May all the IDF soldiers go in peace and return in peace: The investigation of her death revealed that a huge shipment of grenades was faulty and dangerous, and they were recalled from use. Kamay's death saved the lives of many soldiers.

Live Toward Life

Rabbi Tamir Granot

The most important speech in human history is probably Moses's speech before his death – that is, the book of Deuteronomy. What happens there, in that stretch of time when a person knows that soon he will be no more and wants to leave a spiritual legacy for the generations to come?

In the moments before death, there's no more reckoning, no more questions of the here and now. Moses is poised in a liminal space between the present and eternity. At these moments, there is only the distilled essence of life – what remains of all its trials – and a look to eternity, to what comes after my no longer being here. A look that seeks to leave the imprint of the soul, which always remains, even when a person is no more.

The soldiers whose last words are documented in this book are not Moses. The youngest of them are nineteen, the oldest a little over forty. Unlike Moses, they were granted neither prophetic revelation nor a full life of 120 years; rather, they were martyred in the middle of their life's journey.

Even so, these young heroes, who gave their lives for all of us, wrote at the same exceptional moment of their lives as Moses's during his last speech. At the same threshold between the present and eternity, the human and the divine. As they wrote these words, they extracted from their souls' many desires and motions – the essential core.

Over the course of life, we forget the essence, we neglect the essential. Agreeing to push forward without thinking, we complain about trifles and invest in ephemeral pursuits, driven by priorities that do not express our genuine constellation of values.

When a soldier writes a last letter, all this fades away. What remains is the essence of his life, what is most important to him to have remembered, what is most important to him in life itself.

And there's something else. Many of the soldiers in this book think not only of their memory and what they will leave behind them, but also of the people they are leaving behind. They are concerned about the emotional implications of their death for the living and seek to shape their loved ones' attitude toward their loss before it happens. They turn to them and say – pleading, demanding, praying – don't overdo the eulogy, don't be dramatic, be real. Some write: I refuse to let *Am Yisrael* pay the price for my life or my body. And many of them write, in different ways: Don't sink into despair. Be sad, but not too sad. Be strong. Keep smiling. I fought so that you would live. What greatness and nobility of spirit!

This is a nobility deeply connected to their self-sacrifice: Just as these fighters dared to move beyond their individual concerns and sacrifice themselves for their families, for their people, for the sake of eternity, so are they not prepared for their deaths to take up too central a place in the consciousness of those they leave behind.

They sacrifice themselves not just for our very lives, but also for the *quality* of our lives, of all our lives. Live well, they ask. Live with joy. Love. Don't sink into sorrow. This legacy obliges us all.

We should also bear in mind their final directive – to live well – as we approach their words. This book is important, but it is no less important to read it with care, attentive to its effect on us.

Out of all the personal, intimate words in this book, I am certain that everyone can find those that speak to them, give them strength, and uplift them; however, at the same time, I am concerned that an overload of these words, too high a dose, is liable to create an unbalanced perspective on life. This intense collection of dozens of young people's last letters is apt to rattle and upset the equilibrium of our souls.

As the bereaved father of a son, Captain Amitai Granot, who fell fighting courageously against Hezbollah terrorists on October 15, 2023, near Shtula, I am all too familiar with the terrible temptation to live toward death, on the edge, outside of life, so as not to forget and not to disappoint the son who is no more, so as not to get used to that. But I know that's not what Amitai would have wanted. We chose to live toward life, to take from Amitai his light, his greatness of spirit, and his strengths, not his absence.

It's important that we live life without making its center of gravity thoughts of "What will remain after my death?" but rather "What will my future look like, how will I shape it, how can I repair the world through living a long, full life?" Our emotions and moral orientation should not be formed facing toward death, but facing toward life, from within it.

This war has brought us to extremes, situations that heighten awareness of the end. Awareness of the end can elevate life and refine it, but it isn't everything; it isn't life itself.

The fallen had big dreams, lofty aspirations, and also many simple, regular, everyday aspects to their lives, like the rest of us. Their last letters are in fact a pointed reminder of the healthy desires of life, lofty and low, of the ability to dream dreams, to make mistakes, and to live the memorable and the mundane all at once.

So what might they really be asking of us, when we read these words?

Don't live toward death. Live toward life. A meaningful life.

Yonatan Deutsch

Yonatan Deutsch, from Beit She'an, served in the Maglan Commando Unit. He was discharged from combat service after many months of fighting in Gaza, and was killed a week later in a terrorist attack in the Jordan Valley on 8 Av 5784/ August 11, 2024. He is survived by his parents, five siblings, and fiancée. He was twenty-three when he fell.

On October 7th, Yonatan left his home in Beit She'an for the Gaza Envelope, where he fought for three days straight in the fierce battles of Nahal Oz. Four days later, before entering Gaza, Yonatan wrote his last letter in a WhatsApp group with himself.

Yonatan fought in Gaza for many months and came home safely.

A week after he completed his army service, on his way to visit his fiancée Emuna, he was murdered in a terrorist attack on the Jordan Valley Road.

His parents looked through his cell phone and found the letter, which opened with the words "A Word to Myself."

At his funeral, instead of a eulogy, his father, Ori, read out this letter word for word.

In No Way Is This a Goodbye Letter

Yonatan Deutsch

A word to myself,

In no way is this a goodbye letter; it's just a letter to clarify to myself the values that lead me into this battle.

I'm privileged to be a soldier of the Jewish people. There is no greater privilege than this. A dream two thousand years old, and little me has the privilege to fulfill it.

I'm privileged to go out to eradicate the most evil beasts of men humanity has created. ***The images I saw are stuck in my head, and I go out to this battle for them.***

The images I saw are stuck in my head, and I go out to this battle for them: A week after October 7th, Yonatan wrote in his WhatsApp group with himself:

"Taking a moment to write during this whole busy, crazy episode.

It's hard to believe that a week has passed since the moment I woke up on Shabbat morning to a phone call from my teammate and messages about missiles in the south...

We reach the unit as quickly as possible, sprinting to bring out our gear. and going down with whoever managed to come to literally save the Envelope.

At ten in the morning I'm already in Sderot, and starting to realize that this is a much bigger event than I even thought. Let's spare the details, but let's just say that the state of the roads and the amount of murdered people along the way leave nothing to the imagination about the horrors that took place.

We reach Sderot, realize that it's less relevant to be there, and rush with a few teams to Nahal Oz, a kibbutz that was conquered and overrun by terrorists, who are passing from house to house, and you can imagine the rest.

As we drive we start to receive reports of clashes, wounded and dead, some from the unit as well, and we steel ourselves even more....

We reach the kibbutz, divide the area up by teams, and start going from house to house to purge the kibbutz of terrorists. Inside the houses the horrors are even worse. Whole families, the elderly, parents, children...

After no easy fight, the kibbutz is liberated and we can at least breathe a sigh of relief.

We go through the houses and start taking people out of their safe rooms. I don't think there's any better feeling than this anywhere. To tell a family that sat in their shelter with children and babies for ten hours, scared to death of the rioters, 'My name is Yonatan, I'm an IDF soldier, I came to get you out.'

I'm privileged to have a loving, moral, and principled family that pushes me forward and gives me the strength to carry on; it's clear to me that they'll continue the historic ideal of building up the people of Israel in its land, no matter the circumstances.

I'm privileged to have an amazing partner along the way. One who always knows just the right word to say, to give a hug when it's hard, and to always be there for me. One who shows me how you don't need a lot of talk or a lot of publicity, just to always do the right thing. If everyone was like her, we'd have a complete world.

Due to all of these privileges, I'm going out to battle as a proud Hebrew soldier who is privileged to fulfill the ***values of a people thirty-five hundred years old****. Hope I'm worthy of the mission*

and I'm sure I'll do it the best way I can

ובטוח שאני אעשה אותה על הדרך הכי טוב שאני יכול

Don't think there's a more moral and Zionist act than this, and it's something I'm sure I'll never forget. . . .

Since Tuesday when we left the kibbutz all we've been doing is intensive training for all that's required.

It's not hard to find the drive to face what's coming. This time it's not for some vague strategic achievement but rather to make sure that the terrible organization that sent murderers to kill children in their beds won't exist anymore.

That's what drives my friends and I, and we're more focused on our mission than we've ever been in our lives."

Values of a people thirty-five hundred years old: On November 30, 2023, after he and the rest of his commando team were hosted by the Tzuk family in Kfar Aza, Yonatan sent a message to his family WhatsApp group:

"I'm here now on a mission in Kfar Aza, a kibbutz that suffered a harsh blow in this war. One of the residents here spoke with us on the phone and invited us to shower in her home if we want. . . .

Today we discovered that both of that resident's parents were murdered along with two other family members. And still, what she had in mind when she got back to the kibbutz wasn't mourning, but thinking about how to contribute to the good and provide better conditions for the soldiers.

Now it's clearer to me than ever. With this people, it's impossible to lose."

Nave Yair Asulin

Staff Sergeant Nave Yair Asulin, from Karmit, served in the Shimshon Battalion, Kfir Brigade. He fell in combat in the northern Gaza Strip on 10 Heshvan 5785/ November 11, 2024. He is survived by his parents, brother, and sister. He was twenty-one when he fell.

Nave wrote his last letter on November 12, 2023, in the Notes app on his phone. At the time, he was serving on the Lebanese border, and was on the verge of going into Gaza. The soldiers at the Lebanese border were under relentless missile attack. One day, Nave sent a photo of his rifle's sight, aimed at a terrorist at a Lebanese guard post, whose rifle was aimed right back at him. He wrote, "Sis, I could die any day here."

A year later, Nave fell in combat in Gaza. When his parents received his phone, they found his last letter.

In Just a Few Moments You'll Already Be Here with Me

Nave Yair Asulin

The Day After Me

I hope that I'll need to burn these pages at the end of the war and they'll be of no use, but if they are, then at least let them be of good use.

If you read this, it seems that the very worst has happened. But know truly, with a full heart, I'm proud of what I did and I don't regret it for a moment, and I think it's a great privilege to continue the way of our forefathers in the Land of Israel and ***to fight for this soil*** *and avenge the blood of our Jewish brothers who were slaughtered for being Jews.*

Don't sink into sorrow *over what happened, because I'm in a better place, continuing to watch over you from*

To fight for this soil: On Yom HaZikaron, Israel's Memorial Day, in 2023, Nave posted on Instagram: "What does it mean to be a fighter? It's to march on no physical strength left, to think about the blood that was shed over this soil so that we can walk on it, and from there to draw the strength to carry on. To be a fighter is to know that you'd die for the friend next to you and he for you. Why be a fighter then? Because 24,213 people gave up their lives for this land. Because if we don't watch over this country, no one else will."

Don't sink into sorrow: On October 7th, Nave served on the northern border. When he heard about the magnitude of the slaughter, he sent his friends a video, saying: "We've gotten into a difficult situation, but I don't have time to get depressed. In the meantime, let's keep our cool, fix up our gear, get ready for it. We can get depressed when we have time to be depressed."

above where there's no danger and I can protect you better.

I have a request of all who are close to me – family, friends and all the people of Israel – be good to each other, love more, be better friends, be more patient, ***be better people to yourselves and your surroundings****; it could be that this whole catastrophe wouldn't have happened if it wasn't for the divisiveness among our people and what happened to us, for it was baseless hatred that destroyed our Temple and our whole world and led to our exile for two thousand long years, and now that we're back in our land baseless hatred has come again, and with it this grave catastrophe that we've experienced.*

Carry on with life, even if I'm not among you, I'm still with you and I still see you and am with you everywhere, even in the events everyone will have here, with God's help. I'll be there. I promise.

Smile, laugh, love, and take advantage of every moment of life, because you only live once and it's no cliché; it's the real truth.

If I have to die then for the Land of Israel, it's the biggest privilege and ***mitzva*** *a person and more so a Jew can*

Be better people to yourselves and your surroundings: During the fighting, Nave rescued a frightened white cat from ruins in Beit Lahia. He asked his parents to adopt her, because she didn't stand a chance of survival in Gaza, and for them to call her "Lahia." They received the cat during his shiva.

They found it too hard to call her the name of the place where Nave was killed, so they named her "Lily." They're now raising her in their home.

Mitzva: A divine commandment.

*obtain for himself. For they say, "***Someone who saves a single life in Israel, it is as though he saved a whole world,***" so I went to save and protect the whole people of Israel and this land that I love so much.*

I'm taking leave of you, but not for always, just from this material world, which is ***vanity of vanities*** *anyhow. And as absurd as it is for me to say this, in just a few moments and without noticing you'll already be here with me, and we'll laugh over everything that happened*

and I promise you stories that'll seem surreal to you even in the World to Come

ומבטיח לכם סיפורים שיהיו לכם הזויים גם בעולם הבא

Someone who saves a single life in Israel, it is as though he saved a whole world: A paraphrase of Mishna Sanhedrin 4:5. Before Nave went into Gaza, his father told him, "Take care of yourself and wipe out a lot of terrorists." Nave answered, "I'm not interested in terrorists; I'm going out to save hostages, even just one."

In his last phone call with his mother, Nave said to her, "Mom, I found signs of life from the hostages. Be proud of me." Two days later, he was killed.

Vanity of vanities: Quote from Ecclesiastes 1:2.

Itay Amar

Sergeant Itay Amar, from Kochav Yair-Tzur Yigal, served in the Combat Engineering Corps, 601st Battalion, 401st (Armored) Brigade. He fell in the southern Gaza Strip on 9 Sivan 5784/June 15, 2024. He is survived by his parents and two siblings. He was nineteen when he fell.

Itay's last letter was written in the Notes app on his phone on May 6, 2024, just before entering Rafah that same day. About a month later, Itay fell in combat in Gaza along with seven of his friends.

His mother, Lorin, was determined to unlock his phone to check whether Itay left any kind of message behind. Everyone told her that it was a waste of time because Itay wasn't a dramatic type and it wasn't like him to write.

Lorin insisted: "He left one, and how. I know my son. That's what he was like his whole life, keeping me posted. It couldn't be that he'd go in and not leave anything behind. It wouldn't be grandiose, maybe just one sentence, but it would be there."

After a major effort, they managed to crack the phone and discovered a last note, three words long.

The family decided to engrave those three words on Itay's tombstone.

The whole family adopted a screenshot of his last letter as screensavers on their own phones.

Four Words

Itay Amar

Stay happy for me.

תהיו שמחים בשבילי

Stay happy for me: When Itay's parents looked for a photo to send the media after he fell, they couldn't find a photo in which he wasn't smiling. "He was one big smile," says his mother, Lorin. A video filmed before the war shows Itay dancing in an old-age home with his classmate Liri Albag, a surveillance soldier who was taken hostage and only released 477 days later. During a lull in the fighting in Gaza, Itay told his father, "We have to bring all the hostages back home. If not me, then who?"

When he was in high school, Itay became the in-house barber for his friends, and for years, every Friday, his yard would turn into a barbershop and a hangout for the whole gang. Even after his death, his friends kept coming to his family home, and the "barbershop" that continues to operate there has remained a happy meeting place, in fulfillment of his wishes.

Aviad Nayman

Master Sergeant (Reserves) Shlomo Aviad Nayman, from Mitzpeh Yericho, served in the 222nd Battalion, Carmeli Brigade. He fell in combat in South Lebanon on 21 Tishrei 5785/ October 23, 2024. He is survived by his wife, four children, parents, and eleven siblings. He was thirty-one when he fell.

Aviad wrote his last letter in the Notes app on his phone on May 27, 2024, when he was fighting in Gaza.

He came home safely from Gaza, and then took part in the ground campaign in Lebanon, where he fell in battle.

During the war, Aviad told his wife, Shir, that he had left something in writing. Two days after he fell, Shir received his phone from the IDF and found the letter.

"I was surprised when I read it," she says. "The content seemed familiar. At first, I thought maybe he'd already sent this to me once. And then I realized that it was familiar to me because Aviad was familiar to me. He simply captured there who he was and what was important to him to share with the world."

Always Give of Yourself as Much as You Can

Aviad Nayman

1. *Take life easy. Everything is small, everything is transient, but everything matters so much. Pay attention to the little details that most people miss. To the friend who's looking for help and feels uncomfortable asking or the neighbor who writes a vague message on WhatsApp and actually needs help and support.*
2. *People are sensitive even when they don't say it. Take care not to hurt anyone. Even if it seems like correct behavior, it might be that it bothers someone else.*
3. *Know how to hold complexity. Always sort out your own truth and don't give up on it because of external pressure, but do be open to hearing different people's opinions.*
4. *Always try not to be too absolute and not to set the tone, but* ***always give of yourself as much as you can, modestly,*** *without demanding favors in return for the work you're doing.*

Always give of yourself as much as you can, modestly: In Aviad's military company, they made his surname into a verb: "to Nayman."

"It means to get ahold of anything you want for the company, no matter what it takes," explains Yedidya, a friend from his company. "A massage chair for the front guard post on the Lebanese border, an ATV to reach guard posts that the army doesn't allow any vehicles to get close to, a generator and fridge and slushy machine for the waiting area, actual air-conditioning for a site we stayed in in Gaza, and above all – instant coffee and chocolate-coated biscuits, even inside Lebanon, when everyone tries to stick as little as possible into their vest and gets by on dry sausage and tortillas. And all of this to raise our morale."

5. *Money – **don't make an issue out of money**. Even if sometimes there's an abundance and sometimes less, this shouldn't be what guides your life, God forbid. In the end, it's God who makes poor and makes rich and you'll get what is coming to you. In any case, living in **an abundance mindset** opens up the heart.*
6. ***Games, jeeps, and ATVs** – it's all cool and adds spice to our crazy world, but there's really nothing better than those magical moments of Torah study for its own sake. Of meeting goals and knowledge. Not a day goes by without a fierce longing for the time in yeshiva coming over me.*

Don't make an issue out of money: Aviad was the vice president of a real estate company. He understood money, managed big deals, and even partnered in investing in a compound of vacation rentals in his hometown.

"He worked hard but didn't make an issue out of it," says his wife, Shir. "Money was like a game for him, just points you had to collect to get what you want, no matter whether it would get to him or someone else would benefit. If you need to build a synagogue, or establish a farm, then you find the money."

An abundance mindset: "Aviad would show me everything he wrote and ask my advice about phrasing," says Shir. "I would have told him not to write "an abundance mindset" here because it's a phrase that can sound a little mystic and detached from reality, and Aviad was never like that. But he didn't ask for my advice about this specific letter."

Games, jeeps and ATVs: Aviad had an ATV since he was sixteen, and when he grew up he added in jeeps as well, which he and his family used for many off-road trips.

The Nayman family's yard was full of games Aviad brought home: a ping pong table, a shooting range, and a slushy machine that he would take out for the neighborhood kids. Aviad would offer them a trade: a cup of slushy in exchange for learning Mishna.

"He would involve our kids and all the neighborhood children, but he really did it first and foremost for himself," says Shir. "He was like a kid, very competitive; he'd play with the kids and wouldn't let them win. Always playing, always winning."

Shir – ***Every wise woman builds her house****. Wisdom and integrity without* ***impure motivations or distracting thoughts****. If I have an anchor that keeps my head straight in this world, it's you. Your care for our family, even when it's hard and even when you're on your own for most routine tasks with the home and kids, is not at all taken for granted. I'm sorry that I didn't know how to appreciate and repay you for all the good and I'm sorry that my rigidity kept you a bit from moving next to the Sea of Galilee and fulfilling other dreams. I hope the new apartment and neighborhood will be to your liking.*

Hagai – wise and understanding. Sensitive and smart, you understand the world. Besides a healthy soul, God in His goodness gave us the Torah to guide our outlook and daily life. Try and study a lot of the Bible; it connects us to the chain of generations and to the essence of ***a world under the kingship of the Almighty****.*

Tzuriya – you remind me exactly of myself. You have character and special qualities that will help you go far and succeed in anything you want. Make use of it for positive things. Even when it's hard, try and always be connected to the holy Torah and to prayer.

[…]

תשתדלי להיות מחוברת תמיד לתורה הקדושה ולתפילה.

Every wise woman builds her house: Reference from Proverbs 14:1.

Impure motivations or distracting thoughts: Hasidic concept.

A world under the kingship of the Almighty: A reference to the *Aleinu* prayer for enacting a world under the kingship of the Almighty.

[…]: At the end of the letter, after writing to Hagai and Tzuriya, Aviad also wrote the names of his two younger children, but didn't write anything more. "Perhaps by not completing the letter, he didn't fully take leave of us," says Shir. "He hoped that this letter wouldn't actually be put to use. We're waiting for him to come back and complete this section."

Oriya Ayimalk Goshen

Staff Sergeant Oriya Ayimalk Goshen, from Jerusalem, combat soldier in the Givati Commando Unit. He fell in combat in the southern Gaza Strip on 7 Shevat 5784/January 17, 2024. He is survived by his parents and two siblings. He was twenty-one when he fell.

On October 15, 2023, after long days of intense fighting and rescuing residents of Kibbutz Nahal Oz, Oriya filmed a video with a final message for his family.

He sent it to his friend, with the words "Do not open. Only open this and send it to my parents in the event that I don't come back from Gaza."

About three months later, Oriya fell in combat together with his close friend Ori Gerby, during a dangerous mission for which they had volunteered.

The family received the video after his death.
"At the height of the shiva, we received a last will and testament that is very difficult to fulfill," says his mother, Yafit. "But we tried. And we'll keep on trying."

Not as a Catchphrase

Oriya Ayimalk Goshen

What's up? I'm okay; ***don't worry****, love you. Just want to say that it was very good and… I'm okay.*

Don't worry. I want for you to smile and remember only smiles; that's most important. To smile. Everyone says it and it's correct, in the end that's what keeps us, so I just want you to smile.

And really, remember it, ***not as a catchphrase****. I want that with time… keep on smiling, because that's who we are. That's what makes us.*

A smile is our power*, and it's my power too.*

חיוך זה הכח שלנו, וזה הכח שלי גם

Don't worry: The last time that Oriya saw his parents was when he left Gaza for the funeral of his commander, Harel Ittah. Instead of going home, he asked his parents to come join him in comforting the mourners.

Oriya lost many friends and understood how hard it was to deal with grief. When he said goodbye to his parents before going back to Gaza, he urged them, "Please, don't worry about me, worry about them. Support their families."

Not as a catchphrase: Oriya was a man of action, not empty words. He appreciated the story of his parent's immigration from Ethiopia, which entailed sacrifice and an arduous physical effort, and he would talk about it with pride at every opportunity.

In an earlier interview held with him, he said: "I'm now in twelfth grade, and when I sit with my friends and order a burger, I debate with my friends about whether to order fries or onion rings, grape drink or Coke. When my father was five years younger than me, he went from Ethiopia to the Sudan. When you consider that, everything else is so meaningless. There are decisions that change lives, and you need to know how to make good decisions."

A smile is our power: In a message he sent to his friends on October 9, 2023, after the first days of fighting in the Gaza Envelope, he wrote: "Whoa, my brothers!... The images that I assume we all saw are stuck in our heads and probably all of us have a friend missing/dead, but we must not let ourselves fall into the abyss of despair, where it's far too easy to get sucked into in these circumstances. On the contrary! We have to be strong for their sake and for the sake of those we've left at home, who pray for us, and I'm sure it's no less difficult for them."

Eyal Mevorach Twito

Captain Eyal Mevorach Twito, from Beit Gamliel, platoon commander in the 202nd Battalion, Paratroopers Brigade. He fell in combat in the southern Gaza Strip on 12 Shevat 5784/January 22, 2024. He is survived by his parents and five siblings. He was twenty-two when he fell.

Eyal wrote his last letter in his private WhatsApp group with himself on October 30, 2023 during training for the ground entry into Gaza later that week. He didn't show it to anyone. His phone and the letter on it reached his family after his death.

I'm Making Sure That We Stay Here Forever

Eyal Mevorach Twito

What I'm fighting for:

* *My country – the place where my entire past is found. The essence I live for.*

* *My land – the landscapes, the sea, the Negev, the Galilee, and the Hermon. Every piece of earth in my amazing land, the most beautiful place in the world.*

* *My nation – my brothers and sisters, those who live in the land and those outside of it. My extended family who are wherever I go in the world, who will always be by my side during tough times.*

* *My friends – the people I love, who make me happy and push me forward, who are a moral compass but never condescending.*

What I'm fighting for: Eyal answered this question again and again in different ways in the war journal he kept in Gaza. Eyal kept his journal on a secure military tablet and backed up parts of it with images on his phone. The tablet was destroyed in the explosion that killed Eyal, but the family was able to read the parts he backed up on his phone.

On November 7, he wrote:

"Amit, my squad commander, asked me today what's *the* thing that helps me remember why I'm doing all this.

* *My team – my little brothers. The people I love most in the world. The ones I'm willing to take a bullet for, and more important, the ones I'm ready to live with and for. We're all in this together to the very end; we're going out together and coming back all of us together.*

* *My family – my mom, my dad, my grandma and grandpa, my brothers and sisters. My childhood landscape, the people who raised me and grew up with me, and they're everything to me.*

* *My grandfather – who came to Israel in the name of Zionism and built his home in a small moshav [settlement] out of a dream to settle the land. He built a magnificent family and raised them with values of friendship, family, and powerful Zionism. My grandfather stubbornly struggled to get here, I'm making sure that we stay here forever.*

The truth is that the question tripped me up. I've been in this army regimen for such a long time that it's become routine, a matter of habit that I've stopped thinking about in the everyday. I think I've reached the point that I don't have any single thing that reminds me why I'm here. All the reasons combined are my why.

Mom and Dad, my siblings, Grandma and Grandpa, my home, the team, the nation and the country. That's all of it on one foot. I'm grateful for all of these, and I'm ready to fight for them as I do these days."

On November 18, he wrote:

"In a search near us, we found a crazy deposit of weapons. Loads of rifles, explosives, and missiles. Thanks to this operation today we managed to save so many people…

Yesterday we captured Tel al-Hawa. A significant place with a very long history. I remember very well Benaya Sarel's mission here during Operation Cast Lead [one of the most significant battles of Cast Lead, in 2008, in which Sarel and his forces took over a Hamas command center under heavy fire; Sarel fell in combat in Operation Protective Edge in 2014]. The thought that I'm now doing what he did fifteen years ago gives me a lot of strength."

* *My nephew – that beautiful and wise little boy. He will grow up and become a moral man with values. He'll grow up in a better place.*

* *My staff – my fellow team commanders, my sergeant. The people who live with me day by day, who know me and know what I'm going through.*

Those who will always be there at my side, and I'll always be at their side. At regular times and especially at war.

אלה שתמיד יהיו שם לצדי. ותמיד אהיה שם לצדם.
גם בשגרה ובמיוחד במלחמה.

On November 24, he wrote:

"This morning a ceasefire took effect in exchange for fifty Israeli hostages. You can't deny the fact that we played a part in this. I oftentimes feel that I'll only be able to begin to process the magnitude of everything we're doing here when I get back home."

Heroes of Our Present

Lieutenant Colonel Aviran Alfasi, commander of the Givati Brigade

On April 26, 2024, after half a year of nonstop fighting since October 7th, we gathered for an evening to mark the end of this phase of combat for the Tzabar Battalion, which I commanded.

I procrastinated writing my speech until the very last minute. I searched for the right words to mark the occasion. What would I say to the young soldiers who had been fighting so courageously, who had lost comrades in arms, and to the commanders who had led the fighting, risking their lives, to prepare them for the battles yet awaiting them?

And most difficult of all – what would I say to the families of the battalion's fifteen fallen soldiers, who would be sitting across from me in the audience?

When I imagined their proud, grieving eyes, I suddenly knew what I wanted to say.

This is what I said: On occasions such as these, the unit's commander usually quotes the luminaries of previous generations.

He cites **Joseph Trumpeldor; Yigal Allon's** immortal statement that "a people who does not know its past has a meager present and a foggy future"; or David Ben-Gurion's journal entry about the fate of the Jewish state lying in the hands of its security forces.

With your permission, this evening I will choose a different type of speech.

Instead of quoting the heroes of the past, I have chosen to quote the heroes of our present, the last words of young people, soldiers who fell in battle.

Staff Sergeant Adi Leon, of blessed memory, wrote in his last letter: "I'm going out to war knowing that I won't necessarily come back, but I wholeheartedly believe in what I'm doing. We have no other country and now it's my turn to protect it."

Lieutenant Pedaya Mark, of blessed memory, wrote:

"Beloved family, challenging days have come upon our people. We're strong! *Am Yisrael* is strong, the IDF is strong!"

Staff Sergeant Itay Yehuda, of blessed memory, wrote:

"It's important to me to say that I don't regret enlisting for combat for a moment, and it's the best thing I've gone through in my life."

Staff Sergeant Roei Dawi, of blessed memory, wrote:

"If I have to die then only like this. . . . I regret nothing, I had the best service I could ask for. . . . My soldiers are lions, it's a privilege to command them."

Staff Sergeant Shay Arvas, of blessed memory, wrote:

"The truth is that I was happy to do what I'm doing, to save people and protect the country, because that's something I always wanted. Something that was always part of me, ever since I was little, and now I had the opportunity to do it and give of myself to the country. So you should know that all this wasn't in vain and it was worth it. For all of *Am Yisrael* to continue this tradition. And to love the country, because people didn't fall here for nothing, and there are people here that we need to protect."

For me, these are the luminaries of this generation. We called you the TikTok generation, the "What's in it for me" generation, Gen Y, Gen Z, and many other names. This war has proven that only one name befits this generation: the Generation of Courage.

In another ten or twenty years, on a quiet afternoon, your son or daughter will come to you holding their history textbook.

They'll ask you, "Mom, Dad, what's the Swords of Iron War? We learned about it today in class."

After you condense long months of experiences into a sentence, don't neglect to tell them about the heroes of this time period as well. About the new heroes who rose up for us, young people who lived here among us, and fought at our sides, and wrote words with the blood of their hearts, words that will continue to echo here for generations.

Joseph Trumpeldor: Trumpeldor (1880–1920) was a Zionist hero and soldier best known for his bravery and leadership, especially his legendary last stand and reported final words, "It is good to die for our country," at the Battle of Tel Hai, in the upper Galilee, in 1920.

Yigal Allon: Allon (1918–1980) was an Israeli military commander, politician, and statesman who served as a Palmach leader during Israel's War of Independence and later held key government positions, including Deputy Prime Minister and Foreign Minister.

Itay Parizat

Sergeant Itay Parizat, from Petach Tikvah, served in the Shaked Battalion, Givati Brigade. He fell in combat in the northern Gaza Strip on 1 Heshvan 5785/ November 2, 2024. He is survived by his parents and four siblings. He was twenty-one when he fell.

Itay wrote his last letter on his phone on March 17, 2024, before his first time in Gaza – a complex operation in Shifa Hospital.

He sent his letter to his friends Re'em and Ro'i, each with this request: "Listen, bro, I'm sending you and Re'em/Ro'i a message; don't read it. This is only if something happens to me, then you'll send it to my parents and all that. Good?"

When Ro'i tried to reassure him that things would be all right, Itay answered: "I'm calm. It's just in case.... I really am calm."

After Itay fell, Ro'i told his family about the letter. They asked him not to show them the letter before the funeral, but rather that he read it as part of his eulogy.

When Ro'i spoke at Itay's funeral, he read the letter in full, and Itay's parents heard their son's last words for the first time, together with everyone in attendance.

No, I Don't Regret Anything

Itay Parizat

Okay, I can't believe I'm writing a message like this in case something happens to me. How illogical it seems to think about it, and strange.

First of all my family – Mom, Dad, Sa'ar, Noam, Adel, Ariel, the people who will always be there for me.

Mom and Dad, all my life, whenever I needed you were there for me, everywhere and always. I always appreciate it, even when we fight. Always, but always, I love you and you're the most important people to me.

Sa'ar and Noam, my little brothers, I love you more than anything and I was happy to see each of you gradually taking shape and building himself up. I know that I could have been a better brother, more accepting and more patient, but I love you.

Adel, my only sister, I love you. You make me smile whenever I see you. I hope that you'll make the most of yourself in the future and become a successful woman. You're quite an easy target; you remind me of myself, just as a girl.

And Ariel my littlest brother, I'm waiting to come back home and give you a hug. I won't let…

You brought me light, whenever I'm the slightest bit sad or grouchy I look at your photo on my phone and I smile; I really love you more than everyone and you're my light.

Grandma and Grandpa, You've always looked out for me and helped raise me ever since I was little. You always gave me more love than what grandparents usually give. You were a powerful part of my life, especially you, Grandpa Eli, the grandpa who was always there for me whenever I needed, who took me to every game even if it was on the other side of the country. You were always there and you supported me; there's no one else in the world who I love like you, and Grandma, you also always gave support and were there for me. I love you very much.

Grandpa Yechezkel, My godfather, I love you very much; you were there when I needed you; you always looked out for my future and wanted the best for me. I really love you and appreciate you so much for that.

For my second family, my friends from home – ***"The Studs"****:*

It can be said that the best thing in my life was that ***I moved to your class****. I made friends for life; you were always there when it was tough.*

True, I'm in touch with some more than others, but this group is something special and I love you; you're such good people and the best friends I could have asked for.

Klada, Re'em, Afek – the people who have been closest to me since I joined the army; in general we haven't been apart since. I don't have too much to say. I'd just never wish for myself better friends than you.

"The Studs": A WhatsApp group of Itay's friends.

I moved to your class: When Itay was in sixth grade he moved classes, leaving friends he'd been with since kindergarten.

"Not only did he fit in quickly," says his father, Yaniv, "he was also a master at encouraging all the outsiders. Itay was two meters tall and always lifted up anyone who had a lack of confidence. Whoever was near him felt stronger."

The Padbol at 22:00 guys:

We always laughed that we'd never believe that we'd stay so close after school, but in the end you became the people I can't wait to see when I get home. Love you loads (Adar, Henzel, Yarin, and Iddo).

And of course my friends from my platoon, you've become the people I can't live without. This company and platoon are in my blood and I love you.

I know that if you're reading this message, apparently I'm in a quiet place and no longer with you.

I hope that you'll carry on with life, that you'll dare and fulfill yourselves without fear, even if it's scary. No, I don't regret anything I did, especially enlisting in combat and falling for the sake of the country. I'm proud to be part of the Givati Brigade. ***I'm proud to be a fighter,***

and I'm proud to be part of your lives. Love you!

וגאוה להיות חלק מהחיים שלכם. אוהב אתכם!

The Padbol at 22:00 guys: Padbol is a mix of soccer, tennis, volleyball, and squash. "When we were little, we would open a WhatsApp group for everything," explains Itay's close friend Ro'i. "We would play Padbol in the neighborhood and this was the group for setting up who was coming and when. The 'Padbol at 22:00' group was actually a bunch of guys from the second WhatsApp group ('The Studs'), with another few friends that Itay added along the way, who became like family in every respect."

I'm proud to be a fighter: About a week before the war broke out, Itay broke his arm and was on leave from the battalion for a long time. On October 7th he wrote to his commander:

"I want to come help in any way or form, if there's any option of joining up with you. I really want to go in with you and be with you. Just give me the approval and I'm coming. My arm doesn't hurt so much, if that's a factor.

Not at all.

Keep me posted."

Shoam Moshe Ben-Harush

Staff Sergeant Shoam Moshe Ben-Harush, from Hispin, served in the Nahal Commando Unit. He was wounded in combat at the Kerem Shalom outpost on October 7th and succumbed to his wounds on 11 Heshvan 5784/October 26, 2023. He is survived by his parents and five siblings. He was twenty when he fell.

Shoam wrote his last letter on July 3, 2023, three months before war broke out, before embarking on a complex mission, Operation Bayit VeGan to thwart terror in Jenin. Before the mission, the commander prepared Shoam and his friends for the possibility that not all of them would return safely from it. Shoam, who wasn't a big writer, decided to write a last letter then.

On October 7th, Shoam fought in the battle to defend the Kerem Shalom outpost and was mortally wounded.

During his hospitalization, Shoam was unconscious, and his family never left his side. His brother Ori opened Shoam's phone to play his favorite songs for him, and came across the WhatsApp group "Me and Myself," which had just one message. Ori, who wanted to believe that Shoam would wake up and fully recover, didn't read it.

Three weeks later, Shoam died from his wounds. Only six months after Shoam's death, on Yom HaZikaron, Israel's Memorial Day, did the family get together to read his words for the first time.

That's What's Beautiful About the World – That It's Not Beautiful

Shoam Moshe Ben-Harush

The world is twisted, the world is dysfunctional, the world is scary, the world is full of things you don't know. The world is strange, the world is wrong, the world is messed up.

But even with all its flaws the world is beautiful, the world is open for us to discover, the world is open to suggestions – and that's exactly what's beautiful about the world, that it's not beautiful.

I know, it's a bit of a funny sentence, but I love the world I live in. I love the moments that I spend in it, I love all the sensations I get from it, all the experiences it gives me, all the trials it puts me through, because after all, it's our world. This is the world where I spend my life, all my time, and all my moments…

So I want to say something to the world.

You're weird to me, you're strange to me, you're not clear to me, you're different to me, but thank you. Thank you for my living in a different world, in an unusual world, in a scary world, really, thank you!

I don't want to live in any other world. ***I want to live in this world****, in this twisted, dysfunctional world.*

Thank you for putting me through trials and tribulations, ***thank you for giving me strength.*** *Thank you for giving me love, for giving me parents, for giving me friends, for giving me a home,*

for giving me life.

שהם לוי ז"ל

I want to live in this world: Shoam's injury caused irreversible damage to his brain. After his death, his family donated his organs to five people, who continue to live in this world thanks to Shoam.

Thank you for giving me strength: On October 7th, when Hamas terrorists first attacked the Kerem Shalom outpost, there was terrible chaos. Shoam and two of his friends were the first to recover, charge, and return fire, and they waged a heroic battle to halt the enemy.

Ephraim Jackman

Staff Sergeant Ephraim Jackman, from Neve Daniel, served in the Shaked Battalion, Givati Brigade. He fell in combat in the northern Gaza Strip on 15 Tevet 5784/ December 26, 2023. He is survived by his parents and six siblings. He was twenty-one when he fell.

Throughout his army service, Ephraim kept a journal. During the training prior to entering into Gaza, he wrote a last letter in his journal.

On his last visit home, Ephraim left his journal behind, and didn't take it back with him to base as usual.

During the shiva, his brother found the journal, with the goodbye letter at its end, entitled, "Mom."

Mom

Ephraim Jackman

Mom

Mom, if this has reached you, it's a sign that I'm no longer with you.

Mom be strong, I love you very much: Dad, Mom, Elisheva, Binyamin, Yosef Meir, Chana Esther, Avigayil, Rivka Hodaya. And all the grandmas and grandpas, the aunts and uncles, the cousins, and all the friends and all of Am Yisrael. Busy yourselves with moving forward, and don't be too sad. What happened was God's will.

***Please** make the bad lead to something better. **Try to be real with yourselves,** you'll find that way that you'll love and contribute greatly to the world.*

Please: The handwriting of this word isn't clear; it could be "please," *anna*, or "Mom," *Imma*. Please is more likely because the paragraph is all in the plural. If he meant "Mom," this would be the fifth time in this short letter that Ephraim refers to his mother.

Try to be real with yourselves: When he attended a memorial service the month after the death of his friend Eitan Rosenzweig, Ephraim took some time for himself and wrote:

"Deep breaths, step by step, we'll process it yet and know what to take upon ourselves, what's right to do. You have to know how to focus on what interests you, you have to be real and honest, you have to have the ability to say I was wrong, you have to cope.... I hereby take it upon myself not to look at something and say, 'Oops, I didn't notice.' That I'll listen to, and highlight, and find the beautiful points, the depths of the heart."

Serve God from all your heart. Help one another; ***two are better than one.***

To my friends: Counting on you; you have a lot of potential.

Fulfill it! ***Humility, humility, humility.***

תממשו! ענווה ענווה ענווה

Two are better than one: Quote from Ecclesiastes 4:9. When Ephraim was evacuated to the hospital, critically injured, he was still conscious. The first and only thing he asked was if all his friends were okay. A few hours later, he died from his wounds.

Humility, humility, humility: When Ephraim was a counselor in a local youth movement, he and the kids in his group wrote letters to themselves to open five years later.

The five years were up the summer after his death, and his family opened his letter without him. They were astonished to discover that, in response to a question about his character traits, he had written that he was "arrogant."

"Working on this trait was his life's mission," says his mother, Liat, "He died humble, and these were the last three words that he chose."

Asaf Master

Captain Asaf Master, from Kibbutz Bahan, combat soldier and officer in the Yahalom Special Forces Unit and company commander in the Combat Engineering Corps, 601st Battalion, 401st (Armored) Brigade. He fell in combat in the northern Gaza Strip on 2 Kislev 5784/November 15, 2023. He is survived by his parents, two siblings, and a partner. He was twenty-two when he fell.

Asaf wrote his last letter in the Notes app on his phone on October 18, 2023, the day when he and his friends were informed that they would soon enter Gaza. After his death, his letter was discovered on his phone, saved under the title "To My Family."

I'm a Little Scared, but I'm at Peace

Asaf Master

*To my family, that's it, the two weeks are over – of preparations, chaos, staging areas, the Nahal training base, **Tze'elim, Julis,** etc., etc., etc.*

We're going in.

*I didn't plan on writing **something moving that Hanan Ben Ari will turn into a song,** because I'm coming back home in another week and celebrating my birthday at home; don't know what I was thinking.*

But even so, I'll try.

*It must have already been a few days since you saw **updates on the group** and you might have seen on TV that the battalion did something – and you realize that I was part of it.*

Tze'elim: IDF Ground Forces training base.

Julis: Nickname of the Emanuel Army Base, which is also the main base of the Combat Engineers Yahalom Special Forces Unit, in which Asaf initially served.

Something moving that Hanan Ben Ari will turn into a song: Israeli singer Hanan Ben Ari wrote a song "Good Night, Shawn" based on the last letter of Shawn Mondshine, who fell during Operation Protective Edge. Asaf and his partner Gili were very moved by the song, but here Asaf is expressing that he doesn't want to turn into the next song.

Updates on the group: On October 9, 2023, after a few days of intense fighting in the Gaza Envelope, Asaf opened a WhatsApp group named "Asaf's Updates" and wrote: "Hi everyone, I opened this WhatsApp group with a person from every framework that's dear to me. I'll send an update here of what's happening every so often and that everything's okay. That way you can update the others and I'll be able to get fewer messages from the whole world."

You must be sitting around now in panic and suspense, just waiting for the doorbell **ring.**

I want to tell you that I'm the most, most at peace as could be with where I am.

Yes, I'm a little scared, and **perhaps I would prefer to be surrounded by Yahalom soldiers,** *but I'm at peace.*

One day, when Asaf was in the fighting in the heart of Gaza, without his phone, he wrote a letter on paper and gave it to his company sergeant major for his parents:

"You must be losing it out there with the uncertainty and being cut off. . . .

I'll start off and say, first of all, that I'm fine, completely fine.

Tired and confused, a little chafing and a few cuts but apart from that really fine. Morale is high; we know why we're here and we understand [. . .].

Soon we'll all sit together at a proper Friday night dinner.

Keep being strong for me and for everyone.

And remember that I'm taking care of myself and watching over you."

Ten days later, Asaf fell in combat.

Ring: Unclear if Asaf meant the door or the phone. When the army notifies a family of a soldier's death, they ring at the door.

Perhaps I would prefer to be surrounded by Yahalom soldiers: Asaf first fought in the Yahalom Unit, but after he completed his officers' course, his first assignment was in a different unit, as an officer in Battalion 601. He was supposed to begin his next assignment on October 8 and then return to his beloved Yahalom Unit when it ended, but the war that broke out a day earlier changed everything.

Asaf knew that he was not going out to battle with the team and unit with which he trained and that he trusted so well, but rather as an officer in a different battalion. He candidly expresses this concern here, but at the same time, he attests to being at peace with his assignment and his role at this time and place.

I'm proud to be doing what I'm doing, and I know wholeheartedly that I'm doing the most important thing I can do at my age, in this time and place.

I want to say thank you, thank you for bringing me to this point in time, to being who I am.

Without you, I wouldn't be who I am.

[...]

To all my friends, to Omra and Nadav, the team ***Zichriya****, everyone. I love you loads. Thank you for letting me be who I am and feel as free as can be with you. To drink, to laugh, and have fun together.*

Bottom line, everything I've written is a waste of time, no one will read this ever; in another month I'll be starting in ***Chetz,*** *the role of my lifetime.*

I love you all

אוהב את כולכם

Zichriya: Zichriya is the nickname of the boys' group that Asaf belonged to during his pre-military service year at Ayanot Youth village.

Chetz: Chetz is the professional training phase of the combat engineering officers' course where Asaf was designated to serve as team commander.

Shimon Asulin

Sergeant First Class (Reserves) Shimon Yehoshua Asulin, from Beit Shemesh, combat engineering soldier in the 924th Battalion, Harel Brigade, and later in the 646th Paratrooper Brigade. He fell in combat in the southern Gaza Strip on 24 Shevat 5784/ February 3, 2024. He is survived by his parents and nine siblings. He was twenty-four when he fell.

Shimon began writing his last letter in the Notes app on his phone during the war. He had been fighting since October 7th, and after he and his friends were released from reserve duty, he insisted on volunteering to resume fighting. He then joined the Paratroopers Battalion that was fighting in Khan Yunis.

On January 31, before going into Gaza with the paratroopers for a second time, he completed his last letter and told a close friend about it.

Three days later, he fell in combat.

Buy a Karaoke System for the Gang in Dimona

Shimon Asulin

Half my money goes to […] and half to […] ***to rehabilitate the business. Buy a good karaoke system for the gang in Dimona*** *(with my money of course).*

Shmaya, David, and Avraham should feel free to continue fighting. *(I would also continue.)*

Dad and Mom, I love you. Thank you for all the giving, my whole life. You're strong people; there's no point in mourning a lot. Enjoy and keep on living,

To rehabilitate the business: Shimon's brother served as a company commander in reserve duty, and his long months of service and prolonged absence from home affected the new business he had founded.

Buy a good karaoke system for the gang in Dimona: Shimon was part of a close group of about fifteen friends from his high school in Dimona, who often met for song and karaoke nights. After his death, they fulfilled his wish and indeed bought a karaoke set. Ever since, they've been taking it from base to base to raise morale.

Shmaya, David, and Avraham should feel free to keep fighting: Two of Shimon's brothers serve as commanders on reserve duty, and the third is also a combat soldier on reserve duty. They received the news while serving on their respective fronts.

As Shimon requested, the two brothers continued fighting after his death, and the third brother has since completed an officers' training course during his reserve service.

I'm doing great up here and will enjoy seeing you happy, and I'll drop by to cheer you up every so often, when it doesn't interfere with my afternoon nap.

[…] I had a great time with you, I always admired you and the bond with you meant a lot to me.

[…] you have amazing qualities and the power to conquer any goal you want.

To the gang from Dimona, I love every single one of you; you were like a second family to me; keep having fun together…

[…] I really enjoyed our time together; thank you for that. ***You're an amazing girl,*** *live life to the fullest. Any man would want you.*

Until victory, over

עד הנצחון, סוף

You're an amazing girl: About a month before his death, Shimon met a young woman and they started to become close. At the end of a long day hiking together, Shimon added her to this letter, ending it with these words to her.

No Words

Miriam Peretz

Miriam Peretz is an Israeli educator and public speaker who has inspired Israelis and Jews worldwide with her unyielding love for Torah, the Jewish people, and the Land of Israel. Her sons Uriel (d. 1998) and Eliraz (d. 2010) were killed in action serving in the IDF. Her husband, Eliezer, died in his mid-fifties of an illness that developed after the loss of Uriel.

During the Swords of Iron War, wellsprings of words burst open – words of longing, words of love for the land, words that chart a course for life. But even so, there were also major moments when the words were stopped up, leaving a land of no words.

Such was the moment that many families in the Land, mine included, endured.

A knock at the door.

A door that children and guests once entered with joy, a door to a home where two portraits hung at the entrance, of a father and a son – Eliezer, who died of a broken heart after the fall of Uriel, and Uriel, a young Golani Reconnaissance officer, who fell in battle in Lebanon.

A door through which we'd enter into a house bursting with life – music, food, little children, the sounds of living.

And then, a knock.
Silence.

Out of the corner of my eye, I see army uniforms. I understand. They have come with their tidings again.

But this time I won't let them!
I'm not willing to hear the words: *"Today, your son has fallen."*

I close the shutters, lock the door. None go out, and none come in.

I want to vanish, but they make their way inside.

Last words. So very plain, as devastating as they are simple.

I won't let them speak.
I won't allow the words to be spoken.

In desperation, I reach out my hand to shut their mouths. Every moment they do not speak the last words, my son Eliraz is still alive. One more minute, ten more minutes – I want him kept in this world.

And a thought crosses my mind: You're fighting for one more minute! But what did you do with all the minutes you were already granted? After all, every morning you awoke to life. What did you do with that gift, ephemeral and fleeting? And now, you're fighting for just one more minute?

When they could no longer bear the silence forced upon them, I asked them to tell someone else first. I ran out to the yard, pointed at the heavens: "Tell Him!" I cried out in a fury. "Tell Him that His son Eliraz, who loved Him so and dedicated His life to Him, has fallen." I wanted to know how our Father in heaven would receive the news.

And there were no words. Only silence. The world was quiet. The sun gave off light. The world went on. And there were no words to give answer to the question: Why my son, Eliraz? The world was struck dumb. For could there ever be an explanation why his four little children, two-month-old Gili among them, would never see their father again?

And could there be an explanation for the trials I faced, for the devastations I endured?

"And Aaron was silent" (Lev. 10:30). Wordless silence.
Aaron, the man of words, spokesman for his brother Moses, stood facing the death of his two sons: "And Aaron was silent."

The fallen of Swords of Iron, those who stood face to face with the fear of dying whether facing whistling bullets, preparing their gear for a final mission, or riding out into a dark night in their final moments, they carved out last words that chart a course for life. Words of love and gratitude. Words that call on us to make amends, to repair the world.

Words that command by their lives.

"In my blood, Live. In your blood, Live" (Ezek. 16:6)

I came in from the yard.
I saw my two remaining sons, Avichai and Eliasaf.
And for a single moment, I saw something good.

From the depths of pain, I chose, for one moment, to say: Thank You.

Thank You for what remains. For the life that has hold of me.
Thank You for Eliraz's wife and children, for me standing on my feet. Thank You for the Nescafé I drank in the morning, for it was a *nes*, a miracle.
Thank You for opening my eyes. Thank You for still letting me hear the words "Mom" and "Grandma."
Thank You for this heart still beating without stop.

Thank You for the soldiers who stand guard for me at night.
Thank You for our home, for our Land.

And so – *"I shall not die, but live"* (Ps. 118:17).

I shall live in the knowledge that I will never understand the ways of God in the world. But with gratitude for the good that remains. That good must increase.

Gratitude for the eyes that have wept so very much, and choose to see the good. The heart that was broken three times, yet still beats is purer, clarified, and it desires and awaits the Good.

"Depart from evil and do good; seek peace, and pursue it" (Ps. 34:15).

This is the last will of our children, the legacy of life that they have left to us.

For what is life? Life is not how many years you live, but the meaning you pour into them.

Our world was created with speech, good speech, the speech of life.

And we have the duty to carve, out of depths of pain and longing, words of hope and comfort.
Words to heal a broken heart, and pave a path for generations to come.

Aviv Baram

Sergeant Major (Reserves) Aviv Baram, from Kfar Aza, was a member of the first response team in the kibbutz. He fell in the battle over Kfar Aza on the 22 of Tishrei 5784/ October 7th 2023. He is survived by his wife, two children, parents, and a brother. He was thirty-three when he fell.

On the morning of October 7th, at 7:36, Aviv wrote down these last words.

That morning, about 250 Hamas terrorists invaded Kibbutz Kfar Aza. Despite their vast numerical disadvantage, the fourteen members of the kibbutz's first response team went out from their homes to push back the attack.

Aviv kissed his wife and children and said to them, "I love you. There are bad men in the kibbutz. Dad is going to fight them and he'll be back soon."

As he was fighting, Aviv caught sight of some of his friends wounded on the lawn, and ran out to the exposed area to try to save their lives. A band of terrorists lay in wait from nearby rooftops and shot and wounded him.

Aviv managed to take cover behind a tree and continued to fight. When he saw a friend approaching to try to rescue him, he shouted to him to get back so that he wouldn't be ambushed. This saved his friend's life.

With the last of his strength, Aviv took out his phone and wrote three last words on his family WhatsApp group.

Three Words

Aviv Baram

He loves everyone

הוא את כולם אוהב

He loves everyone: As Aviv wrote these words, he was on the cusp of passing between life and death. "He wrote about himself in the third person," explains his wife, Heli, "as if he's no longer in his body, not totally here. He was a people person, a person of tremendous love for everyone as they were, and his last three words are the essence of the person he was."

Nadav Cohen

Staff Sergeant Nadav Cohen, from Haifa, served in the 77th Battalion, 7th (Armored) Brigade. He fell in combat in the southern Gaza Strip on 21 Adar Bet 5784/ March 31, 2024. He is survived by his parents and two siblings. He was twenty when he fell.

Starting on October 7th, Nadav fought in Gaza for ninety consecutive days until he was injured and went home for a short leave to recover.

On January 19, the day before he went back to fight, he wrote his last letters. He saved them in a computer folder under a random string of letters and numbers as a title, so that no one would open it by mistake.

That day, he messaged his friend Peleg, asking him to open the secret folder in the event that something would happen to him. That is what Peleg did.

Nadav left behind four letters in the folder. This is one of them.

The Decisions That Demand the Biggest Sacrifice

Nadav Cohen

To my beloved pre-army program,

To the fifty most amazing people I ever met, students and staff alike.

I begin each letter with its bottom line, and so far in every letter it's the same: I love you.

Thanks to you, thanks to every one of you, my pre-army year was what it was – ***the most meaningful year of my life****.*

This is a year during which I learned more about myself than I could have imagined, a year in which I stood facing challenges I never imagined I'd face, and a year in which my environment pushed me to improve and challenged me intellectually, but more important, ethically, in a way that I never thought I would have to contend with.

My peers – which I spent most of my time this year with – and I were required to use our heads a little, open our eyes,

The most meaningful year of my life: Nadav had many dreams for after his army service, but one thing was absolutely clear to him: He wanted to join the counseling staff in his pre-army preparatory program, "Be'eri." His younger sister Roni joined the program in his footsteps.

Nadav's family is currently working on founding a new pre-army program in his name.

and see how complex the reality we live in is and try to pave lives for ourselves within this complex maze, to understand what we believe in and what we're willing to sacrifice in order to live those beliefs.

And on the other hand, these friends sometimes put me into pigeonholes of their own, which taught me about myself, taught me about my friends, and deepened my relationship with the truly incredible people who surrounded me this year.

To the senior staff, who always took care to guide us during this surreal year, to give us advice and be a support for us in moments of crisis, but on the other hand knew how to give us independence, allow us freedom of action at every junction we came across, and always knew how to challenge us to see all the sides of reality when we were trying to understand where to place ourselves within this surreal reality.

Thanks to you, thanks to each and every one of you I explored my beliefs and values in depth and changed or deepened them in a sincere, grounded way. Thanks to you I improved – not in a way I felt from day to day, but in retrospect I can't even imagine the person I was before the program.

You helped me get to know myself deeply, you helped me to improve, and most of all you made this year enjoyable in a way that I couldn't imagine possible.

I came to the program with high expectations following my brother's experience – expectations that I wasn't sure would be met, and you exceeded those expectations in an exceptional way and granted me the most enjoyable, meaningful, and maturing year I ever had.

I chose to enlist in combat service and to live the beliefs and values that I acquired here in the program – ***despite all the difficulties this entails*** *– and in the end I had to pay the ultimate price.*

But that's how it is in life: The choices that go hand in hand with the values you believe in, especially as idealistic graduates of a pre-army program, will inevitably be the most difficult choices, the choices that demand the biggest sacrifice.

I ask you to continue to make these choices, looking at each choice like this not as a sacrifice, but as an opportunity to fulfill the values you believe in, make an impact, make change, improve your environment, but above all ***experience, enjoy, and keep up the magic*** *that's known as "the class of year 6."*

Love you on astronomical levels and believe in you

אוהב אתכם ברמות אסטרונומיות
ומאמין בכם

Despite all the difficulties this entails: Nadav had asthma and didn't originally seem destined for the tank corps. He was a brilliant young man who took university courses in philosophy while he was still in high school, and he was on track for a prestigious intelligence program.

During his year in the pre-army program, Nadav chose to give up on that opportunity in order to enlist as a combat soldier.

Experience, enjoy, and keep up the magic: "Nadav gobbled up life," says his mother. "The family joke was that in our next home, we wouldn't keep a room for him. He just needed a parking spot, a shower, a car, and a prepaid gas card."

Nadav's WhatsApp description was "If I had a clone, I would get twice as much done." The family had this engraved on his tombstone.

Liron Snir

Captain Liron Snir, from Ofra, team commander in the Golani Brigade's Commando Unit. He fell in combat in the northern Gaza Strip on 9 Kislev 5784/ November 21, 2023. He is survived by his parents and two siblings. He was twenty-five when he fell.

On November 19, just before his first entry into Gaza, Liron had a long telephone conversation with his father. Afterward, when he was on the bus from the staging area to the Gaza Strip, he took some time to himself and wrote his last letter on his phone.

Two days later, Liron fell in combat.

And Now It's My Turn

Liron Snir

It's finally happening, ***I was already starting to lose hope that we'd go in****, and thank God I have the privilege of taking part in the war and being inside Gaza, to fight, to restore the honor of the IDF and Am Yisrael, and above all to make sure that it's* ***Never Again!***

What was is not what will be, and we're stronger, better, more moral, and have the authentic claim over our life and our existence in the Land of Israel. And now is the time to state this clearly to ourselves and to the whole world: Am Yisrael is strong, and what happened to Hamas will happen to whoever tries or wants to hurt us.

The people have power, have unity, and it hurts that God needs to show this to us the hard way. But I'm happy that all this strength and unity is coming to light and going into action.

And now it's my turn – to be, to fight, to dare, and to command this team at this time, in this war. I will fulfill this role with might and humility and I will lead the

I was already starting to lose hope that we'd go in: When war broke out, Liron and his soldiers were immediately sent to prepare for going into Gaza. In those weeks, a few teams went into Gaza while Liron's team remained on standby in the staging area. On his own initiative, Liron traveled to the command center every evening to get up-to-date and to put pressure on the unit commander to have them join in the fighting.

Never Again: A slogan coined in response to the Holocaust.

team in battle. We are strong and full of power, happy for the privilege to participate!

If, God forbid, something happens to me, I love my family, and I am who I am thanks to them. We must remember ***to live in greatness****, to love life, and to always add good to the world. To make people happy,* ***to see the weak and help them.*** *To smile at people, to throw out a kind word. The aspiration is to be good, good to all – and it doesn't cost us a thing to be good and do good.*

I'm happy with my life and with what I did and who I was, for the sake of my people, for the sake of whoever was around me over the years on whom I succeeded in having a positive influence.

We need to be good and do good!

אנחנו צריכים להיות טובים ולעשות טוב!

To live in greatness: After Liron fell, his family founded a non-profit organization in his memory to contribute to causes that were close to his heart: aid for lone soldiers, for Torah study, and financial aid for families in need. The organization is called "to live in greatness," *Lehiyot b'Gadlut.*

To see the weak and help them: At the beginning of the war, Liron and his twin brother Alon were eating out in Be'er Sheva when suddenly a siren sounded. When everyone ran toward the public shelter, Liron ran in the opposite direction. When Alon peered out from the shelter, he saw Liron protecting an elderly couple in wheelchairs with his body, calming them down and watching over them until the danger passed.

Daniel Kastiel

Master Sergeant Daniel Kastiel, from Beit Shemesh, served in the Maglan Commando Unit. He fell in combat in Zikim on 26 Tishrei 5784/October 11, 2023. He is survived by his parents, four siblings, and a partner. He was twenty-four when he fell.

Daniel wrote his last letter on October 8 in the Notes app on his phone, in the heat of battle, between a day of intense fighting in the Gaza Envelope and continued fighting in other arenas.

At the same time, Daniel sent a WhatsApp message to his partner, Maya: "Pray for the wounded... so many good people, salt of the earth, are falling here in battle, it cannot be believed. My commander died today; he managed to kill about seven [terrorists]. And two other fighters from the unit along with him."

Three days later, Daniel fell in combat in a confrontation with terrorists on the Zikim shore.

His family only managed to track down Daniel's phone three months after his death. His brother Raziel found Daniel's last letter on the phone, but couldn't bear to open it. Yoni, the oldest brother, gathered the whole family into the living room, opened up the letter, and read it out for the first time.

Know That I Went Out with My Head Held High

Daniel Kastiel

I love every single one of you. You're my pride in life; there was no place where I was ashamed to come from the Kastiel family. I can't even describe how much I love you.

[…]

All my friends and family – I love you; thank you.

Always keep smiling and be strong and everything's okay. I'm happy and proud of this path and it was all out of choice; there's no one happier than me.

"Though I walk through the valley of the shadow of death, I fear no evil, for You are with me."

Know that I wasn't afraid and ***I went out with my head held high.***

Though I walk through the valley of the shadow of death, I fear no evil, for You are with me: Quote from Psalms 23:4.

I went out with my head held high: On October 7th, when battle raged most fiercely, when the true scope of the horrors started to emerge, Daniel stopped for a moment to record a message to his brother Raziel, a member of the Border Police who had also been called up and was fighting in a different sector:

"Razi, what's up. man? Listen, I'm just reminding you to stay focused. Don't tell people what's happening, what the situation is, who's dead, and who's dead. . . .

Whoever's dead is dead. It's over. We keep moving forward.

And we have no other land

והלכתי עם הראש למעלה ואין לנו ארץ אחרת

Encourage your friends, keep morale high, stay sharp, eyes up. No phone, no Instagram, no nonsense, my brother.

Be focused, finger on the trigger, eyes up. Got it? Don't focus on what was and what will be, and don't listen to stories, don't watch videos; it's not good for your soul.

Come see my guys – they're all locked in, all cheerful, all smiling. No one is turning his phone on at all. We're ready. You also have to be ready; got it?

Charge up your guys, rile them up, keep your eyes up. That's the situation. From here we keep moving forward.

Got it? Get going, take care of yourself."

In Daniel's last words, in his last letter, he attests to fulfilling what he had asked of his brother: to keep his head up.

And we have no other land: Reference to the Ehud Manor song.

Ben Zion Falach

Captain Ben Zion Falach, from Nitzanei Oz, combat officer in the 202nd Battalion, Paratroopers Brigade. He fell in combat in South Lebanon on 29 Elul 5784/ October 2, 2024. He is survived by his parents, two brothers, and a partner. He was twenty-one when he fell.

Ben was part of one of the first IDF ground forces to enter Lebanon. On September 30, 2024, a few hours before he went in, he wrote his last letter. Two days later, he fell in combat.

His family found the letter in the Notes app on his phone, entitled "The Real Test."

In Hard Times You Need Strong People

Ben Zion Falach

There's a feeling that everything I've trained for up to now is going to be put to the test in this maneuver.

To go into Lebanon??? Who even dreamed of that?

What a privilege to take part in it. I still haven't absorbed that out of the entire IDF, I'm participating in the first maneuver in Lebanon.

I'm ready, the team is ready; more time would always help like they always trained me, but there's no possibility of waiting anymore. We need to finish up this story now, as quickly as possible.

There's a feeling that everything I've trained for up to now is going to be put to the test in this maneuver: on October 7th, Ben rushed to fight in the Gaza Envelope. After a few days of intense fighting, he wrote down his thoughts for himself on his phone, entitled "Swords of Iron – My Journal":

"7:30 Saturday morning Dad wakes me: 'Terrorists from Gaza have invaded Israel and they're walking the streets and shooting people.'... I find myself saying goodbye to my family on Shabbat morning without knowing when I'll see them again.

We drove to the base, and on the way we heard people on the radio who are trapped in their homes, and about the party in Be'eri. I'm still not managing to process the situation, but thoughts of 'War, let's go' are running through my head – everything I've been talking about for the past five years from in the dormitory to today, all the lectures, the war stories, the training, will now be put to the test. Now is the moment of truth.

We reached the division at Kerem Shalom and met the company that took the hit there. To see a company broken like that is tough.

I'll remember this period for the rest of my life. In another five hours I go into Lebanon to perform the mission of my lifetime. I'm sure that we'll do it in the best way possible and that we'll withstand the challenges.

I'm going in for the sake of putting an end to the threat to the residents of the north, so that they can go back to their homes.

For the sake of my team, who I love and am prepared to die for.

A lot of experiences and, at the same time, the names of the dead keep flowing. Roi Nahary was the commander of the parallel platoon in my training course. I was supposed to be under his command. What an amazing man. Adam was in my platoon in training and then with me in the room in the squad commander course, and then in a role in the company. His was the hardest for me to accept. I never lost such a close friend before

At times like these, you understand what's really important. All the baloney, the niceties, the apologies melt away and you deal with what's really important. Maybe, if something good will come out of this whole war, it's that we'll all go back to understanding that."

For the sake of my team, who I love and am prepared to die for: Ben commanded a team of relatively new paratroop recruits; they had been in the army for only ten months when they entered Lebanon.

Ben was killed during a search in a village in Lebanon. Based on IDF warfare doctrine, Ben was supposed to be the third to enter the building, but he couldn't bear the thought of sending his soldiers to endanger themselves ahead of him. He decided to go in first, and was attacked by terrorists who shot him in the heart. In his final moments, he managed to return fire and report the encounter on the radio. None of his soldiers were harmed.

For the sake of ***my family,*** *so that they can live in a more peaceful country.*

For the sake of my Rotem, who I love so much, who's the woman I want to marry and live my life with.

And for my own sake, for I have been preparing to carry out this mission for so long.

If only the situation were different, but at the moment, this is the reality.

And to contend with hard times you need strong people

בשביל להתמודד עם תקופות קשות צריך אנשים חזקים

My family: All three Falach sons fought on the northern border at the same time.

Amit, the oldest, fought as a paratrooper on reserve duty, and the twins, Ben and Yonatan, entered Lebanon on the first day of the IDF's ground operations there, fighting in two adjacent villages.

Yonatan, a fighter in an elite unit, called his parents after a fierce battle to let them know he was okay. He didn't know that at the same time, in a village just seven hundred meters away, his twin brother had fallen in combat.

The Words After the Last Words

Iris Haim, palliative nurse

In his final days, a person lies dying in his bed. More often than not, he's no longer capable of speaking a word. Often, he passes away suddenly, exactly when his family members have left the room, leaving them with a sense of loss at missing the chance to say goodbye and not saying what they wanted to while they still could.

As a palliative care nurse, I have been accompanying terminally ill patients and their families for many years. Years of observing goodbyes, disappointments, missed opportunities, frustration, and grief at not getting to say the last words that we wanted to.

If I only could, I would tell him that…

I would tell him that I love him. I would ask his forgiveness. I would sing for him again – that song that always brought us together. I would thank him for everything. I would tell him that it's a shame he won't see my son get married. I would tell him that I forgive him.

While the patient was still alive, living inside a sleeping body, unconscious, I would encourage his family to talk. Standing with them next to the sickbed, I would suggest that they tell him how much they love him, that they give him a blessing for his old-new journey through this world.

And sometimes, even after the person's soul had departed the body, I would say to the family: "You can still tell them everything. He's here; he can hear you." I understood, even then, that the person's spirit was there with us in the room. I understood that they could say anything, and the words would get to where they needed to go. The deceased would hear them and take them with him.

To speak to someone who's unresponsive is no easy task. To stand in front of him and pronounce words, or even to sit there without talking, but speaking silently from the heart, isn't something we're used to. We feel silly, awkward, anticipating a response that doesn't come.

"Yes, he's listening; he's here with us," I would prod the family who found it difficult to approach a relative who could not give them a response. I would encourage them to move past their discomfort and speak anyway, because words unspoken hurt even more. They make it hard for us to say goodbye. And when we don't say goodbye, we're left with a sour taste of loss, of everything we didn't tell our loved one in time, of everything unsaid.

I've seen terminal patients who were near death for a long time and only left the world after someone close to them visited and said, "Thank you," "Goodbye Dad," "Goodbye Mom."

And what does the patient say for himself? What are his last words?

Mostly – the long silence of deep exhaustion. A painful sigh. A request for help. Loving eyes seeking rest. Sometimes, "Am I about to die?" "Stick together," "I love you," "I'm all out of strength," "Let me go," "Thank you," "Goodbye."

The last words that I take from my son Yotam are the words he sent us in a video filmed by terrorists in the Hamas terror tunnels where he was held captive.

"Mom, Dad, I'm strong," he said with a slight smile playing on his lips, placing a strong, tattooed hand on his heart.

Only after Yotam fulfilled his purpose in this world did I understand that there is really no such thing as last words. There are the final words spoken out loud and audible to the ear, but afterward there are many more words that can be said to our loved ones, and can be heard from them, even when they're no longer physically here.

As I see it, Yotam can see and hear me. And I – when I'm in the right state of mind, attuned and aware – I can hear him, too. Already during the first days of shiva, when I got into bed and turned out the light, I felt a delicate energy in the bed. I thought maybe the cat had crept inside, but no, it wasn't the cat; it was something else. It was Yotam's energy. And to this day, sometimes, when I'm attuned to my senses, I know how to recognize that energy: a kind of delicate tingling on the upper back, to the left side, directly opposite my heart, that tells me that Yotam is here.

I know clearly that Yotam is here, because I'm always talking about him, showing his picture everywhere I go, telling stories about him. When I do that, he's present. I listen to old WhatsApp messages from him every once in a while, so that his pleasant voice stays with me. Even when I choose my words, I don't say that Yotam is "gone." He is here, here when I feel him without touch, when I listen to him without hearing a sound. If we make space for the presence of our loved ones who have fulfilled their purpose in this world, if we're attuned to them, if we recognize that they're still with us, we can always continue talking to them, and nothing really comes to an end.

Yossi Hershkovitz

Sergeant Major (Reserves) Yosef Haim Hershkovitz, from Gevaot, served in the 697th Battalion, 551st Brigade. He fell in combat in northern Gaza on 26 Heshvan 5784/ November 10, 2023. He is survived by his wife, five children, parents, and five siblings. He was forty four when he fell.

On November 6, four days before he fell, Yossi sat down in a house that had been destroyed in Beit Hanoun and wrote in a small pocket notepad.

He handwrote seven letters in that notepad: to his parents, to his wife, Hadas, and to each of his five children.

Yossi sent the notepad with his brother-in-law Ori, who was fighting with him and was due for a short leave home. Ori gave the notepad to Hadas that same day, and she was surprised to discover that the notebook was full of goodbye letters and not "how are you's" or greetings.

Hadas understood that Yossi felt that the end was near. She gave his parents the letter intended for them that day, but held onto the letters for her children, and read only excerpts to them.

When Yossi fell that Friday afternoon, their children read the letters in full.

This is his letter to his parents.

Like Standing at Mount Sinai

Yossi Hershkovitz

Mom and Dad, how are you? Thank God I'm totally fine, and by the grace of God I am privileged to take part in the effort to protect God's humbled people, who are now able to begin to hold their heads high, thanks to the scale of ruin and destruction that the wicked Nazis are now experiencing.

***"I walk upon ruins, Mother,"** is a poem written during the Yom Kippur War, and now, so right. We're walking upon ruins, searching and destroying.*

***It's not easy to be there on the home front.** I feel that your prayers for me help a lot and your many merits protect me. Keep praying with all your might, because great miracles are happening here.*

"I walk upon ruins, Mother": This poem was written by Sergeant Reuven Politi, who served in the Egoz Commando Unit and fell in the Yom Kippur War; Idan Raichel set it to music.

It's not easy to be there on the home front: Yossi was the principal of the Pelech School for Boys in Jerusalem and, aside from his own family, he left behind six hundred students on the home front. He cared deeply about them, fought for them, and also drew strength from them.

In one of Yossi's phone calls with his wife, Hadas, during the war, she felt that he needed encouragement. She asked the staff at his school to send him a few words, and in response his students wrote sixty heartfelt letters to their admired principal.

Yossi received the letters in Gaza and sat up all night with his headlight, reading and weeping. When his friend told him to go to sleep he answered, "I need this. I need strengthening."

The next evening, he was killed.

You raised me to give, without taking in return *and not just out of habit, and thank God I have the privilege of being part of an amazing people, and among amazing men who give their all for the sake of the people.*

How much slander has been said about this people this past year *and how much is it all lies and falsehood. We're all here fighting shoulder to shoulder, all* ***as one person with one heart,*** *and the feeling is like we're standing at Mount Sinai.*

I'm glad you raised me this way, charting a path for me where the question is not what do I deserve, but how can I, at each and every moment, give more for the sake of my people and country.

Love and miss you, אוהב ומתגעגע

Yossi יוסי

You raised me to give, without taking in return: "You raise a child for years and then let him go on his way, and you don't know what's left," says his father, Yaakov. "And then you read the letter, and discover that it's all there."

How much slander has been said about this people this past year: In the last video Yossi filmed for his students from inside Gaza, he made one request of them: "I ask you here, as a personal favor, not to do any badmouthing (*lashon hara*) of *Am Yisrael*. Nothing. Don't say a bad word, don't go back to what was before – nothing. There's no Left, no Right, no ultra-Orthodox – nothing. There are Jews.

The Hamas Nazis made no distinction and had no interest in how you voted and what you think. It's a self-reckoning that we must always bear in mind. Not to speak *lashon hara*. During the time of King Ahab, Israel won all its wars because they never spoke badly of each other. That's how we'll prevail. Here, if anyone even tries to ignite that kind of discussion, everyone silences him. We're not talking about that anymore – we're talking about how good we are, and how much we chose good. Our people have so many merits right now. So many heroes who have given their lives."

As one person with one heart: The rabbinic Midrash on Exodus 19:2 describes the children of Israel's encampment at Mount Sinai in these terms.

Reef Harush

Sergeant Reef Harush, from Kibbutz Ramat David, served in the commando training school of the Commando Brigade. He fell in combat in the southern Gaza Strip on 27 Adar Bet 5784/April 6, 2024. He is survived by his parents and sister. He was twenty when he fell.

Reef wrote his letter before the first time he went into Gaza. On March 7, 2024, he came home for Shabbat, and when his father emptied the pockets of Reef's uniform before he did the laundry, he found a folded piece of paper with a letter in Reef's handwriting. He peeked inside and then held onto it.

A month later, Reef fell in combat. About an hour after he received the news, his father read the whole letter for the first time.

For That Old Woman Who Thanks Me and Cries

Reef Harush

Why am I risking my life? *They've done it before me and they'll do it after me.* ***And for that old woman who thanks me and cries*** *I'm willing to sacrifice my life.* ***And for my family*** *to sit in quiet and comfort, that they should know that behind them is an enormous army who will watch over them as long as we're still on our feet.*

Why am I risking my life: In conversations with his parents, Reef admitted that he was afraid of death. He didn't show the letter to anyone; his father just happened to find it. "Reef was aware that he was risking his life," says his father. "He probably wrote this to encourage himself a moment before going out to battle."

And for that old woman who thanks me and cries: Reef was known in the kibbutz as the "old ladies' favorite." He is likely referring here specifically to a one-hundred-year-old woman from the kibbutz who loved him very much. When Reef asks himself why he's willing to risk his life, that old woman is his answer.

And for my family: Mere days before he fell, Reef sent his father his bank password "so you'll have it."

The Shabbat before he was killed, Reef asked each of his family members individually to come and visit him at his base. In retrospect, the family refers to that visit as "Reef's goodbye party."

Much of it is from a personal drive. Toward my enlistment I came to many realizations. And slowly, slowly, my why and my real reason get stronger. Why did I decide to give up my comfort?

*At first, I didn't really understand the meaning of this and it all sounded cool to me and all good. Today, what keeps me going with these things is my team, because we're all in the same s***, and also, to be honest, I've gotten used to it.*

I tried my best and this is where I've gotten to. I said that if I'm already joining the army,

then to a place that'll bring out as much as possible and maximize

אז למקום שיוציא ממני כמה שיותר וימקסם

Gilad Nitzan

Staff Sergeant Gilad Nehemya Nitzan, from Shilo, served in the Givati Commando Unit. He fell in northern Gaza on 19 Heshvan 5784/ November 3, 2023. He is survived by his parents and six siblings. He was twenty-one when he fell.

After three days of intense fighting in Nahal Oz, when he was training for the ground operations in Gaza, Gilad called his good friend Ahia. He said, "First of all, I love you very much. Don't get too worked up about what I'm about to tell you; everything will be all right. But I'm sending you a recording and if, God forbid, anything happens to me, send it to my parents."

Ahia answered him: "Bro, seriously? Soon we'll be sitting together as usual; why are you being so dramatic?"

That was their last conversation. Two weeks later, Gilad was killed.

The family received the news fifteen minutes before Shabbat started. On Saturday night, after the funeral, Ahia tearfully told them that Gilad had sent him a recording, but because Gilad had told him not to listen to it while he was alive, he never downloaded it onto his phone, and it got deleted.

Three weeks later, the family received Gilad's personal belongings from the army, including his phone, which was locked. His parents hoped that they would be able to open it so that they could find the recording. "We tried to figure out what the code could be. What would he use? Gilad was a sweet person, not a wise guy. We tried 2580 – the middle row of numbers on the keypad, the simplest code possible. And it worked."

I'm Sorry I Left So Soon

Gilad Nitzan

Dear Mom and Dad, beloved family,

I am recording this message before they collect our phones so that I can say a few final things in case something happens to me during the war.

First of all, I love you more than I can say. It's hard to describe how much I appreciate you and how much love I feel toward you.

I also want to ask forgiveness for anything I might have done. If someone is upset with me, angry at me, or feels that I committed to doing something for him and didn't carry it out – I ask for complete forgiveness.

And if I feel any kind of anger toward someone, they should know that I completely and absolutely forgive them, I have no hard feelings toward them, nothing. I forgive everyone.

My requests are **to be buried in Shilo,** *and that all the savings* ***should go toward Torah study and settling the***

To be buried in Shilo: Gilad's parents didn't hear his message until after the burial. They had debated whether to bury Gilad in the military graveyard on Mount Herzl, because "after he was killed, he became a child of the entirety of *Am Yisrael*," or in Shilo, where he grew up. "We knew that for Gilad, Shilo was his soil, the place where he was born, planted trees, and struck roots." They decided to bury him in Shilo, fulfilling his final request without realizing it.

Savings should go toward Torah study and settling the Land of Israel: In light of his request, his family took all his savings and used them in his memory, to establish: "Gilad's room," a study room in Gilad's yeshiva, Yeshivat Avinoam; a lookout on Mount Keida; a Torah scroll; and an educational center in his name.

Land of Israel, *to promote those values in the world. I truly believe that this is the most important thing of all.*

I love you in a way that's not to be taken for granted. And I'm sorry if I ever caused pain to my parents, my family, my friends, really, I'm sorry from the depths of my heart.

I really love you, each and every one,

I'm sorry I left so soon.

סליחה שהלכתי כל כך מוקדם

I'm sorry I left so soon: Gilad's motto in life was: "In a place where there is nobody, strive to be a somebody, and in a place where there are people, be the first." (See *Pirkei Avot* 2:5)

On October 7th, Gilad fought in Nahal Oz, and after three days of fighting he spoke with his mother, Yehudit, and happened to mention that he had broken his finger. Yehudit was happy to hear of his injury because she thought that now he would come home, but Gilad explained that he had broken a finger on his left hand and he used his rifle with his right hand, so he could keep on fighting.

During the fighting in Gaza, Gilad and his fellow company members were the first to sweep a suspicious area. They were confronted by terrorists, and Gilad was killed alongside his battalion commander, Yehuda Cohen, and his good friend, Yonadav Levenstein.

Ben Zussman

Sergeant First Class (Reserves) Ben Zussman, from Jerusalem, served in the Combat Engineering Corps, 601st Battalion, 401st (Armored) Brigade. He fell in combat in the northern Gaza Strip on 20 Kislev 5784/December 3, 2023. He is survived by his parents, sister, and brother. He was twenty-two when he fell.

On October 7th, on his own initiative – without being called up for reserve duty – Ben left home to fight. While he was on the bus on the way to his base, he wrote his last letter.

He sent the letter to two close friends and asked each of them: "Read the message and show it to everyone only if the worst comes to pass and something happens to me."

On the morning of his funeral, Ben's family received the letter, together with additional personal messages to his friends and family.

I Don't Allow You to Sink into Sorrow

Ben Zussman

I'm writing you this message on the way to the base.

If you are reading this, something has probably happened to me.

As you know me, there's probably no one happier than me right now. Not for nothing was I really on the verge of fulfilling my dream so soon.

I'm happy and grateful for the privilege to defend our beautiful land and the people of Israel.

Even if something happens to me, I won't allow you to wallow in sadness. I had the privilege of achieving my dream and my goal and be sure that I am watching you from above and smiling a huge smile. ***I will sit next to grandpa and fill in a few blanks,*** *each one of us will share our experiences and what changed from war to war. Maybe we'll also talk a little politics; asking him for his opinion.*

As you know me, there's probably no one happier than me right now. Not for nothing was I really on the verge of fulfilling my dream so soon: About a week after October 7th Ben was supposed to join the Shin Bet, which was his dream. Because of this new role, he had been taken off of reserve duty. Ben joined the fighting on his own initiative, without being called up.

I will sit next to grandpa and fill in a few blanks: Ben grew up one street away from his grandfather, who passed away two years before Ben was killed. Saba Shmulik grew up in ultra-Orthodox Me'a She'arim, and chose to enlist in the army. He served in the reserves for many years, and was very proud of Ben and his combat service. Ben knew that as someone with strong opinions, his grandfather would make a fine partner for endless discussions in Heaven.

If the worst comes to pass and you are sitting shiva, turn it into a week of friends, family, and joy. Have food, definitely meat, beer, sweet drinks, nuts, tea, and of course, Mom's cookies.

Laugh, listen to stories, meet all my friends that you haven't yet met. Honestly? I envy you. I would have loved to be sitting there to see everyone.

[…]

Another very, very important point. ***If the worst comes to pass and I fall captive,*** *dead or alive, I am not willing for a soldier or civilian to be harmed because of any deal for my release. I do not allow you to conduct a campaign or struggle or anything like that. I am not willing for terrorists to be released in exchange for me.*

In no way, shape, or form. Please do not violate my words.

I'll say it again – I left home without even being called up to reserve duty. I am filled with pride and a sense of duty, and I always said that if I have to die, I hope it will be in defense of others and of the country.

"Jerusalem, I have set guards over you. / May the day come when I'll be one of them."

"ירושלים, הפקדתי שומרים, יום יגיע ואהיה אחד מהם"

If the worst comes to pass and I fall captive: During those first chaotic hours of October 7th, Ben followed the Arabic news on Telegram. Even before the rest of the country realized the severity of the situation and how many people had been taken hostage, Ben knew full well what he was getting into, and composed this message to his family.

"Jerusalem, I have set guards over you. / May the day come when I'll be one of them": A quote from the song "Keeper of the Walls" by Dan Almagor (written in 1977), which was Ben's favorite. Ben grew up to be a proud Jerusalemite. True to his nature, on the way to fight for the Gaza Envelope, he envisioned Jerusalem.

Adi Baruch

Staff Sergeant (Reserves) Adi Odeya Baruch, from Kiryat Netafim, operations sergeant in the Judea Regional Brigade. She was killed by a missile on her way to the base in Sderot on 27 Tishrei 5784/ October 12, 2023. She is survived by her parents, two siblings, and boyfriend. She was twenty-two when she fell.

After Adi's death, her mother Orit went through her personal computer and found over a hundred poems she had written, meticulously arranged by date and subject. One poem caught her eye: "And If I Should Ever Die."

The poem was written in January 2023, nine months before she was killed, at a time when she had lost two close friends to untimely deaths.

The poem was published after her death and was set to original music over twenty times.

Every Once in a While, Smile at the Clouds

Adi Baruch

If I die

Before my time,

I want you to celebrate life

Not to mourn my death.

I want you to wake up every morning

With a smile on your face and longing in your heart,

And don't let a single second of your life go to waste.

See the world for me, *appreciate every little moment,*

If I die: On October 7th, Adi didn't get called up, but she did everything she could to go on reserve duty. When she was called up to run the operations center in Sderot in the first days of the war, she came right away.

As she left the house, she saw how difficult it was for her parents and said to them, "I know you're worried about me, but you're the ones who raised me for this my whole life. What did you think I'd become, a chicken? I want to thank you for letting me apply what I learned from you, and I hope to raise my kids this way too."

About an hour later, mere minutes before she reached the operations center in Sderot, Adi was hit by a rocket and killed.

See the world for me: Adi's keen eyes knew how to capture what others didn't see. When she was fifteen, she fell in love with photography, and when she finished her army service she opened a photography business and gave it her all.

And every once in a while, smile at the clouds *– I'll be there.*

I'm sorry for the grief I caused,

Know that I'm in a good place.

I miss you,

And I love you very much.

מתגעגעת ואוהבת מאוד.

When her commander wanted to start a camera-based operations center in Sderot soon after the start of the war, he declared: "There's only one girl who can do it with me, and if she doesn't come, it's not happening."

And every once in a while, smile at the clouds: Adi had a special love for clouds, and they often starred in her photos. One of the poems her mother found after her death is entitled "Clouds of Cotton Candy."

Roee Negri

Major (Reserves) Roee Negri, from Tel Aviv, combat team commander in the Lotar Counter-Terrorism Unit. He fell in combat in Kibbutz Be'eri on 22 Tishrei 5784/October 7th 2023. He is survived by his wife, parents, and two sisters. He was twenty-eight when he fell.

Thirty-nine days after Roee's death in battle, his wife, Shai, received a message from Roee's close friend from his unit, Oron Pariente, who had finally left Gaza after weeks of continued fighting: "I need to keep a promise I made to Roee."

The Negri family gathered in their living room and Oron read them a transcript of his final conversation with Roee on the morning of October 7th.

Early in the morning of October 7th, Roee realized the enormity of the moment, and even before he received orders, he called up his anti-terror reserves team for duty.

As Roee and Oron geared up at the Adam facility enroute to the Gaza Envelope, they were notified that their friend Ben Rubinstein had fallen in combat in Sderot.

"It was the first time that Roee and I had ever lost a friend from the unit in combat," says Oron. "And we knew that we were charging, eyes wide open, into the very same event where he'd been killed. And we were speaking on the phone with a friend who was fleeing the Nova festival and he described seeing hundreds of terrorists, and we were getting videos on Telegram, and the sense was that, right then, they were beating us, and we were literally going to fight for our home. We're a very cynical unit and we always make fun of everything, and last letters are totally not our thing, but suddenly it was real. This was our first real war."

In the few minutes when they awaited transport to Be'eri, Roee and Oron sat on the curb behind the armory. They asked each other if they had written a last letter, and neither had.

Roee said, "I don't really know what to write. Instead of writing, come, you tell me and I'll tell you, and in another two weeks we'll laugh at one another."

Mere hours later, Roee fell in combat in Be'eri.

Oron heard about Roee's death but kept on fighting. He fought nonstop until the afternoon of October 8. When the battle was decided, the first thing Oron did was to take up pen and paper from one of the ruined homes there and write out from memory his last conversation with Roee, word for word.

What Am I Supposed to Say Here? Do I Sum Up My Life?

Roee Negri

Oron: Okay, your turn.

(Now there was a long silence and I smiled at him.)

Roee: You understand? That's the reason I don't want to write, I have nothing to say. What am I supposed to say here? Do I sum up my life? Do I give instructions for what's next? Do I tell the ones I love that I love them? That's all clear from before…

Oron: I think you just say it and in two weeks I'll give you feedback about what wasn't as good.… Come on, tell me what you're afraid of.

Roee: I'm not afraid of what will happen to me.… ***I saw what a sudden death does to the people around you,*** *and I don't want that to happen to the people around me. I saw families fall apart over the loss of one member, and that's not what the people around me deserve. No one I know deserves for me to do that to them. I got married less than two months ago, bro; I'll be an uncle any minute! This is no time to go. I'm here to protect my home and to return to it.… Why are you looking at me like that?*

I saw what a sudden death does to the people around you: Two and a half years before the war, Roee lost his good friend Ido Kontes, an officer in the elite Shaldag Unit, in an accident. Roee had talked to him on the phone just minutes before his death, and Ido's death had a profound effect on him and their friends.

Oron: Because you're giving me a great motivational clip, but I need to hear what you want to say if…

Roee: What to say…. Say that all I want is for them to go on living the best there is. I want to say something cliché and kitschy about Shai, but less than two months ago I promised her the whole world and now you're asking me to say that I'm not going to keep a word of it….
From my perspective nothing interests me so much as the fact that I want only the best for her; she deserves to have a family that she loves and to be happy. I want my family to always be surrounded by so much love that it can compensate for any loss they'll have from me, as if I never left. I want my friends to manage to accept a second loss within two and a half years, just like we managed to accept the first loss. What can I tell you? On the whole I want my name to bring up a smile and joy and not tears and sadness – just like a commander is measured in his absence, I think that I did enough in life to ensure happiness even when I won't be here. I want memories of me to be happy things that are fun to talk about, that when they talk about Roee Negri in the past tense it'll be at a get-together with beers and laughter, and not tissues and ice-cream.

Oron: What do you want to tell Shai?

Roee: This is like the moment to say move on, but that's too obvious…. There's nothing you can surprise her with; I love her. She's the first thing that comes to mind with every decision here and I guess the last thing I'll think about. You know this. I fell in love with her from the first moment and now I'm sorry for every moment that I didn't tell her that I love her.

> *You understand that anything I could tell you now, I said to her less than two months ago under*

the wedding canopy on the best day of our lives, right? She's the best thing that happened to me and sometimes I wonder to myself how it happened that specifically I had that privilege…

Oron: Something to the family?

Roee: I don't even know how to start with that… I only have trivial things in my head. The thought of you talking to them crushes my heart; you know how special our bond is.

And even though I'm only twenty-eight, I think that we've shared a whole life's worth of experiences. It's just never enough. I was raised by the best couple of parents in the country and I hope I raise my kids like they raised us – I think that says it all.

I'm sure that my family will be strong. My parents will keep this family going and my sisters will make the family bigger with their new families, ***and either way, I'll be part of it.***

Oron: Something for ***"The Blacks"****?*

Roee: I love you even though you're all beasts and I'm just a twig.

I didn't think at first that this is what would become of that gang – we're crazy guys, and

And either way, I'll be part of it: Three weeks after Roee fell, his sister Gal went into labor. There were complications and Gal almost passed out. In terrible pain, Gal asked her mother to put Roee's dog tag around her neck. Gal gripped the dog tag tightly and gave birth safely to her daughter Ori.

"The Blacks": Roee's gang from the unit nicknamed themselves "The Blacks."

looking back, I can't imagine my life without you. ***But I knew that I had to bet on black, I saw it as soon as we got there, and because of you, we lost the money.***

Oron: ***Truthfully, did you propose early so you wouldn't lose the bottle?***

Roee: Let's go; shut it already, you dummy.

Oron: You realize that you basically called me up, right?

Roee: Yeah.

Oron: ***Are you scared?***

Roee: ***No.***

But I knew that I had to bet on black, I saw it as soon as we got there, and because of you, we lost the money: This was an inside joke between Roee and Oron about a time that they were in a casino together.

Truthfully, did you propose early so you wouldn't lose the bottle? Five years before the war, Roee's friends ("The Blacks") placed bets on who would get married first. They placed their notes inside a bottle along with three thousand shekels.

Years later, Roee proposed to Shai earlier than expected. His friends always teased him that he would do anything for money.

Are you scared? No. When he arrived at Be'eri with his team, Roee saw that some of the fighters were shocked by the horrific sights there, and said to them, "The gates of Hell have opened. We're not looking at the bodies. We're here to save civilians, our people. We're fighting for our home."

Roee was killed when he was the first to break into a house to save the people held hostage inside. When he was accosted by a terrorist there and shot, Roee pushed his team back and saved them with his body.

Oron: Do you want a long hug?

Roee: Yeah.

At Roee's funeral, his father, Shmulik, eulogized him:

"When Roee went from house to house in Be'eri to save the hostages there – children, mothers, babies – and got to the cursed house, if God had whispered in his ear:

'Roee, if you go inside, you're dead. If you go inside you're dead, Negri,' would he go in or not?"

In response, completely spontaneously, Roee's whole team standing around the grave roared together: "He'd go in!"

*

Mere hours before his last conversation with Oron, when Roee said goodbye to his wife, Shai, she asked, "Are you scared?"

Roee was quiet for a few moments, and then he answered, "Yes."

Acknowledgments

When we began this journey we didn't know how complex and sensitive our work on this book would be.

Thank you to Koren Publishers for eagerly supporting this project and being its best possible home. Thank you to Matthew Miller, publisher, and Yehoshua Miller, CEO, whose immediate response to our idea was, "First of all, yes. The rest is details." Thank you for your responsiveness to every request that made this book as dignified as it deserves to be. Thank you to Reuven Ziegler, who believed in this project and pushed it forward; you were the wind at our backs.

Thank you to Oriya Mevorach, editor-in-chief of the Hebrew divisions of Maggid Books and Toby Press, who became a true friend and partner and guided us at each crossroads with wisdom, sharp insight, and never-ending sensitivity, and with a sense of humor that kept us all sane. Thank you as well to managing editor Caryn Meltz, who led this project with professionalism and attention to every small detail, and with great sensitivity and respect for the families of the fallen. Thank you to Sara Daniel for translating these very hard words and keeping the meaning of the original Hebrew words and to Laurie Novick who edited the letters and also maintained the voice of the original Hebrew letters.

Thank you to Shmooel Lasry for making a complex layout seem effortless and elegant, for creating portraits that honor the book's heroes, for precise suggestions and patience during the endless rounds of corrections. Thank you to the brilliant Yoni Salmon for the illustrations at the back of the book.

We wanted a cover that would give readers a sense that this book, despite its heroes having fallen in combat, is full of snippets of life. Thank you to Tani Bayer, for the artistic cover concept and design and for your sensitivity to the essence of the project. Sincere thanks go to Tomi Mager for her professionalism in typesetting the intricate layout, to Mitchell Schneider for marketing, and to Gabi Rosenthal, Koren Publishers' printing expert, who accommodated our crazy ideas. Thank you to the proofreaders, Debbie Ismailoff and Esther Shafier. Many thanks to Achinoam Blau, who volunteered to help with the translation project and was in direct contact with each bereaved family to ensure that every word was accurate, and to Ashirah Firszt, who with great professionalism and devotion made sure we obtained all the necessary permissions.

Thank you very much to Leah Marmorstein-Yarchi and Yael Mesika-Maimon from the Ot.Hayim Initiative, who devotedly shepherded the manuscript through the process of generating each last letter's final words in the handwriting of the fallen. Thank you very much to the Ot.Hayim designers: Noa Cohen Salmon, Shikma Benmelech, Efrat Chen, Miriam Ben Yitzhak, Shir Carmi, Nerit Zeliger, Shaked Mori, Hila Stern, Naama Meir Isaac, Atara Ozen, Efrat Yitzhakov, Hodaya Korkos, Moria Hadassa Rotenberg, Neria Ben Moshe and David Mandel.

And thanks to you, dear readers, who opened your hearts to read these words.

To learn more about the fallen,
visit the book's website.
Scan the code: